Please renew or return items by the date
shown on your receipt

www.hertsdirect.org/libraries

Renewals and
enquiries: 0300 123 4049

Textphone for hearing
or speech impaired   0300 123 4041

OAK.

HOW TO DEVELOP A
BRILLIANT
MEMORY
week by week

50

Proven Ways
to Enhance
Your Memory

DOMINIC O'BRIEN
Eight Times World Memory Champion

This edition first published in the UK and USA 2014 by
Watkins Publishing Limited
PO Box 883
Oxford, OX1 9PL
UK

A member of Osprey Group

For enquiries in the USA and Canada:
Osprey Publishing
PO Box 3985
New York, NY 10185-3985
Tel: (001) 212 753 4402
Email: info@ospreypublishing.com

1 3 5 7 9 10 8 6 4 2

Printed and bound in Great Britain

A CIP record for this book is available from the British Library

ISBN: 978-1-78028-790-4

Watkins Publishing is supporting the Woodland Trust, the UK's leading woodland
conservation charity, by funding tree-planting initiatives and woodland maintenance.

www.watkinspublishing.co.uk

Contents

Introduction

I have come to believe that many, if not most, of us have the potential to become "memory champions". Having trained members of the public through game shows and lectures, as well as in impromptu meetings (for example, in restaurants), I always find that people are amazed by the way in which their memory power appears to be instantly transformed. All they have done to achieve this is implement the basic principles outlined in this book.

How to Develop a Brilliant Memory Week By Week aims to unleash the power of your memory by showing you these simple techniques in bite-sized chapters. You are never too young nor too old to acquire these skills. If you are new to memory training, then I have no doubt that you, too, will be amazed at how easily you can learn these methods and how quickly you can employ them.

To get the most out of this book I recommend that you perform the exercises and tests, which are contained in most steps. You will require a notebook for writing down your answers and for keeping a note of your scores.

The scores fall within three categories: Untrained, Improver and Master. Adding up your score for an exercise will tell you which level you have achieved. In each case, the scoring bands reflect the relative difficulty of the individual exercise. The Untrained score indicates the points I would expect someone to attain without using any memory techniques. The Improver score is the category you are aiming for; and the Master score shows a truly outstanding result. Within this scoring system, you can see how well you are doing compared to someone with an average untrained memory, and how much your own memory is improving from one step to the next. Don't worry if you score poorly to begin with or if you find certain exercises more difficult than others – some of them are designed to be quite tricky! You can repeat the exercises and tests as many times as you like: memory is a faculty that is always improved by practice. The exercises and tests will not just enable you to memorize particular types of information, but will also sharpen your memory in general.

Chapter 1 is designed to evaluate your existing memory as well as introduce you to the basic memory tools that you can use on a day-to-day basis. In chapter 2 you will develop these basic principles for use in a wide range of practical applications, such as How to Remember Names and Faces, and Speeches.

Chapter 3 will develop your memory power to a more advanced level. You will be combining many of the techniques already acquired in order to memorize more complex sets of information.

By Chapter 4 your memory will be powerful enough to tackle the final, very challenging steps. The book concludes with some short tests which I am confident will reveal a great improvement from the initial assessment you took in Step 1.

Take as much time as you need to complete each step. I hope you will find my methods challenging as well as fun to learn.

Memory Tools

- *Step 01* **How Good is Your Memory?**
- *Step 02* **Visualization and Observation**
- *Step 03* **Acronyms**
- *Step 04* **Turning Numbers into Sentences**
- *Step 05* **The Body System**
- *Step 06* **Association: the First Key**
- *Step 07* **The Link Method**
- *Step 08* **Location: the Second Key**
- *Step 09* **Imagination: the Third Key**
- *Step 10* **The Journey Method**
- *Step 11* **Concentration**
- *Step 12* **The Language of Numbers**
- *Step 13* **The Number-Rhyme System**
- *Step 14* **The Alphabet System**

Memory depends on three basic processes: making something memorable, storing that item in the mind, and recalling it accurately at some future time. Before you can begin to improve your memory you must have faith in it as a perfectible faculty. We may speak of having a memory "like a sieve" – yet this is not in the same order of reality as being balding, or colour-blind, or pigeon-toed. As you begin to use the memory techniques in this chapter, you will find that your ability to recall facts, numbers, objects, events, places and people gradually sharpens.

This chapter begins with some word, shape and number tests to help you to evaluate your current memory power. You will learn some basic stand-alone techniques, such as Acronyms and the Body System, that are useful for memorizing small and simple sets of information.

Then we look at developing the key skills of association, location and imagination. I will introduce you to effective memory techniques including the Journey Method, a filing system for storing items you wish to remember, and the Number-Shape System, a way to recall a sequence of numbers from four-digit PINs to historical dates. I will guide you as you learn these methods and practise them in the various exercises.

01 **How Good is Your Memory?**

Whether you feel your memory is unreliable or performing reasonably well, the chances are that it is already in fairly good shape. But it is likely that no one has shown you how to access its true potential. Self-doubt may have crept in as you become conscious of forgetting people's names, where you left your wallet, or that new PIN for your credit card.

This first step will measure how good or indifferent your current memory power is through several tests. Write down your answers and keep track of your scores in your notebook.

Don't worry if you score poorly at first, as I am confident you will make rapid progress after just the first few steps of your 52-step journey to a perfect memory.

TEST 1: Words

Allow yourself three minutes to study the following list of 20 words. Write down as many words as you can recall. The order is not important. Score one point for each word you can recall correctly, then move on to the next test.

> TREE   TIME   FACE   PIPE
> CLOCK   MOUSE   ENGINE   PLANET
> THUNDER   NECKLACE   WARDROBE   CATERPILLAR
> GARDEN   TREACLE   PICTURE   HARNESS
> SLEEP   APPLE   OCEAN   BOOK

TEST 2: Number Sequence

Study the following sequence of 20 digits for three minutes. In this test the order is important. In your notebook write down as many numbers in the correct sequence as you can before a mistake is made. Score one point for each correct digit. This is "sudden death": in other words, if you recall all 20 digits but the fifth digit is incorrect, your score is four. Good luck!

5 0 3 6 7 4 4 0 9 2 8 2 0 5 7 6 7 1 2 9

TEST 3: Shapes

Take three minutes to look at the following sequence of 10 shapes. Memorize them in the running order shown below, from 1 to 10. Then turn the page where you will find the shapes reproduced in a different sequence. Follow the instructions you find there to complete the test.

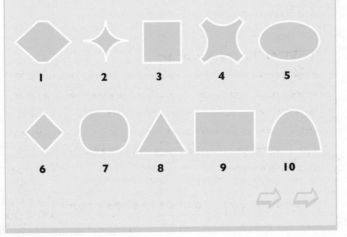

 *test continued*

Below you will see the same shapes you have just memorized, but in a different order. Try to number them in their original order (that is, as shown on the previous page, but without referring to that page). Score one point for each correctly numbered shape.

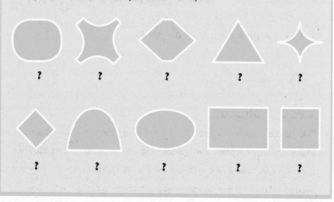

TEST 4: Binary Numbers

Allow yourself three minutes to memorize the following sequence of 30 binary numbers, then in your notebook try to write down as many of these numbers as you can before a mistake is made. Score one point for each correctly remembered binary number. Again, this is "sudden death": if you recall the first five digits correctly, then make a mistake on the sixth digit, your score is five.

1 1 0 0 0 0 0 1 1 0 1 1 1 0 1 1 0 0 1 1 0 1 0 1 0 1 0 0 1 1

TEST 5: Playing Cards

Take three minutes to study the following 10 playing cards, then try to repeat the exact sequence in your notebook. As with the numbers, this is "sudden death". Score one point for each card you can recall before a mistake is made.

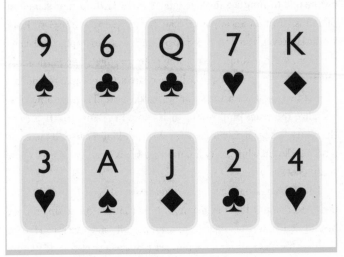

Score *Add up your scores from the five tests to arrive at a total.*

Maximum points: 90   Untrained: 20+   Improver: 35+   Master: 70+

If your score is above the Improver range, then you have great memory potential – expect superb results by step 52. Don't worry if your score is below the Untrained range: once you start following these steps you should notice impressive progress straight away, and I am in no doubt that your memory will be in great shape by the end of this book.

02 **Visualization and Observation**

Throughout this book I ask you to picture or visualize various objects, faces and places. Some people worry that because they are unable to produce in their mind's eye a faithful representation of items, such as an apple or cow, then these techniques will not work. However, you don't need to produce a photographic replica of the item: all that is required is simply to imagine some particularly memorable aspect of whatever it is you are attempting to visualize.

Let's say you want to picture a panda bear. There's no need to visualize the exact proportions of its nose in relation to its ears or the glint of the sun catching its fur. Just think of a cartoon image of a big black and white fluffy animal with black eyes and maybe some sharp claws.

I find when I am chasing through a list of, say, 100 words, and trying to commit them to memory, I concentrate on getting a flash of one element of the object. For example, all I may see for the word shoe is a shoelace, or for a telephone I may get a split-second picture of the keypad on my own phone.

Remember, the word "imagine" does not only mean, *to form a mental image*, it can also mean *to devise or contrive*. The image you create is specific to you – it exists only in your mind and is not real outside of this perception.

There are techniques for developing powers of mental imagery, and the more you exercise your memory the stronger your inner eye will become.

EXERCISE: Visualization through Observation

This is a great exercise for enhancing the visual side of your memory as well as developing powers of observation.

1   First, take any household object near to hand such as a telephone, vase, kettle or radio. Let's suppose you choose your kettle: study it for about 15 to 20 seconds to observe as many aspects of it as possible.

2   Now close your eyes and recall as much about that object as you can in your mind's eye. To begin with, all you may recollect is the shape of the kettle's body and the curve of the handle. When you've run out of ideas, open your eyes and take in more detail, such as the shape of the spout or the manufacturer's name.

3   Close your eyes once more and add your new observations to your original mental picture. Then open your eyes again to observe more detail. Keep repeating this pattern of open eyes – observe – close eyes – review, until you have absorbed as many features of the kettle as you possibly can.

4   Now, without looking at the object, try to sketch these memorized features in your notebook. When you have exhausted your visualized recollections of the kettle, take one final viewing to notice if there is any more detail that you could add to your stored mental picture file.

03 **Acronyms**

You are most probably already familiar with using Acronyms as a memory aid. An Acronym is a word formed from the first or first few letters of several words. For example, NATO is an Acronym for North Atlantic Treaty Organization. The Acronym is spoken as a word, rather than a series of letters each with its own pronunciation. Here are some more examples:

JPEG	*Joint Photographic Experts Group*
RADAR	*Radio Detection And Ranging*
SCUBA	*Self-Contained Underwater Breathing Apparatus*
UNICEF	*United Nations International Children's Emergency Fund*
WHO	*World Health Organization*

EXTENDED ACRONYMS

One popular form of Acronym is when a sentence or verse is created from the first letter of each word to help us remember certain pieces of information in sequence. This is known as an Extended Acronym. For example, to remember the colours of the spectrum – Red, Orange, Yellow, Green, Blue, Indigo, Violet – British readers will find the following ditty familiar:

RICHARD OF YORK GAVE BATTLE IN VAIN.

EXERCISE: Extended Acronyms

Take a look at the following two examples of Extended Acronyms:

- ***Sergeant Major Hates Eating Onions***
  Great lakes of North America:
  Superior, Michigan, Huron, Erie, Ontario

- ***Help Five Policemen To Find Ten Missing Prisoners***
  Bones of the lower limb:
  Hip, Femur, Patella, Tibia, Fibula, Tarsals, Metatarsals, Phalanges

Now see if you can memorize the following two sets of data by creating your own Extended Acronyms. Be imaginative and use exaggeration and humour to make your own Acronyms memorable.

- ***Volts = Amps x Resistance (Ohm's Law):***
  Hint: Make a saying from the three letters V, A and R.

- ***Order of the nine planets from the sun:***
  Mercury, Venus, Earth, Mars, Jupiter, Saturn, Uranus, Neptune, Pluto
  Hint: Again, make a saying from the first letters of each planet in order.

I will be asking you to recall your two Extended Acronyms in a moment, but first, let's have a look at a variation in the Acronym method, one that helps us to remember numbers.

04 **Turning Numbers into Sentences**

On February 18th 1995 at NHK Broadcasting Center, Tokyo, Japan, Hiroyuki Goto recited Pi by memory to 42,195 decimal places. He did this to set a new world record. Pi denotes the ratio of the circumference of a circle to its diameter and is approximately 3.1415926. It makes for the perfect test for remembering numbers as the ratio forms a transcendental number: in other words, there are an infinite number of decimal places that can be memorized.

In Chapter 4 I will explain how it is possible to memorize hundreds of binary numbers using my Binary Code and a system for grouping six or more digits together combined with the Journey Method (see Step 44).

But for memorizing a smaller sequence of numbers, such as your social security, passport or telephone number, mnemonics can be used. A mnemonic is any device that aids memory. In the previous step we looked at Acronyms, which are probably the most commonly used form of mnemonics. We can use a technique very similar to that used to create Extended Acronyms to memorize a small sequence of numbers. Each digit determines the number of letters in each word in the sequence. For example, you could use the following mnemonic to memorize the first few places of Pi: 3.1415926

HOW I WISH I COULD ENUMERATE PI EASILY
(3) (1) (4) (1) (5)   (9)   (2) (6)

EXERCISE: Creating Sentences from Numbers

Try making Sentences out of Numbers to memorize the following two sets of data. Use your imagination and be as inventive as you like. Remember, the digits denote the number of letters in each word:

1   *PIN - 3316*

2   *Passport number - 154244625*

Review the two Extended Acronyms that you created in the exercise on page 19, followed by the two Sentences out of Numbers that you devised in the above exercise. Cover the top half of this page and write down the answers to these questions in your notebook:

1   *What is the four-digit PIN?* ⇨ *Score 10 points*

2   *What is Ohm's Law?* ⇨ *Score 10 points*

**3   *What is the order of the nine planets from the sun?*
    ⇨ *Score 20 points***

4   *What is the passport number?* ⇨ *Score 20 points*

Score You need to recall each word or number correctly and in sequence in order to score any points:

Maximum points: 60   Untrained: 10+   Improver: 30+   Master: 50+

05 **The Body System**

In this step I am going to offer you a quick-fix memory system for those occasions when you want to instantly memorize something. The Body System is a very simple but effective way of storing a few items such as a shopping list. It works by associating parts of the body with key imaginative mental pictures of whatever it is you want to remember. The more vivid or exaggerated the picture the better, because that will help to fix it in your memory. There are no hard and fast rules with this system, but I would suggest you limit it to store no more than 10 items. You do not need to use the same 10 body parts labelled on the diagram opposite. And you can work through a list from your head down to your feet, or vice versa.

Let's say you need to remember the following 10-item shopping list: blue paint, dog biscuits, newspaper, flashlight, prescription, chicken, toothpaste, bananas, shampoo and alarm-clock batteries.

I picture putting my **foot** into an open pot of *blue paint*. I imagine a *dog* jumping up at my **knee**. A rolled-up *newspaper* is sticking out of my pocket (**thigh**). A *beam of light* is shining from my **belly button**. A *prescription* is stuck to my **chest**. A *chicken* is perched on my **shoulder**. I have *toothpaste* smeared around my **mouth**. My **nose** is shaped like a *banana*. My **hair** is covered in shampoo lather. In my **hand** I am holding a loudly ringing *alarm clock*.

With a little imagination I can quickly commit to memory a list of items. The following exercise lets you try out this system for yourself, by asking you to remember a list of 10 shopping items.

EXERCISE: Using the Body System

The diagram below labels 10 key body parts. Make associations between each body part and each of the 10 items on the list below.

When you have created all 10 images, review the entire sequence in your mind. Then cover this page and see if you can write down all 10 shopping items in your notebook.

Score 10 *points for each correctly remembered item.*

Maximum points: 100   *Untrained: 20+*

Improver: 50+   *Master: 90+*

Hair

Nose

Mouth

Shoulder

Chest

SHOPPING LIST

CARTON OF MILK
BUNCH OF GRAPES
RICE
VITAMINS
PASTRIES
ORANGE JUICE
FILM FOR CAMERA
FRESH FLOWERS
BLACK PEPPER
VACATION BROCHURE

Belly button

Hand

Thigh

Knee

Foot

06   **Association: the First Key**

Association is at the heart of developing a perfect memory. It is the mechanism by which memory works. The brain comprises billions of neurons or nerve cells that are connected together in a maze of pathways, allowing an infinite number of permutations of thoughts and memories. Therefore, it is feasible to suggest that any two thoughts, ideas, words, numbers or objects can be linked easily no matter how contrary their nature, and in a rich variety of ways. All you need to do is to allow your thoughts to radiate freely.

For example, how does your brain process the two objects chalk and cheese? What do you associate with these words? Chalking a picture of cheese on a chalkboard? Prodding cheese with a stick of chalk to test its firmness?

We tend to think of an object not by its dictionary definition but rather by the notions which we associate with it. When I hear the word "frog" I don't automatically compute *a tailless web-footed amphibian*; rather, I think of a pond, tadpoles, a scene from a fairy tale, footage from a TV nature documentary, and much more. When you see the word "snow" you don't perceive it as *atmospheric vapour frozen in crystalline form*; more likely you have personal associations, such as building your first snowman, a skiing holiday, a famous film, snowball fights, and so on.

With so many possible associations and a vast network of interconnected brain cells to act as a conduit for these linked thoughts, it is surely possible to find an association between any two sets of information. How would you link frog and snow together? A frog made of snow? A frog leaping through snow? A frog skiing? With just a little imagination the permutations of links are endless.

This conveniently takes us to the next step, or should I say, the next link on the chain to a perfect memory … the Link Method. But before we take that next step, let's exercise those lively neurons of yours by playing a game of free association.

EXERCISE: Free Association

One at a time, say each of the following 10 words and immediately write down the first word or thought that pops into your head. There are no rules and no points to be scored. This is merely a way of limbering up for the Link Method by allowing your mind free range to think whatever it wants to think. Try not to deliberate for too long on any of the words. Your first associations will be the strongest and most significant.

TRAMPOLINE   TELEPHONE   BRAIN   MOON   DREAM
RELATIVES   SNOWFLAKE   BRIDGE   TEDDY BEAR   MEMORY

07 **The Link Method**

The Link Method is a simple and effective method for memorizing any sequence of data, whether a shopping list, or a set of names, concepts, objects, directions, and so on. All that's required is an unleashing of creative imagination.

How could you remember the four objects, *hand*, *butter*, *magnet* and *atlas*, in sequence using the Link Method? Imagine putting your *hand* into some *butter*. From inside the butter you pull out a

---

EXERCISE I: Using the Link Method

Using your powers of creativity and association, memorize the following list of five words using the Link Method:

PAPER   WINDOW   SNAIL   CAR   GUITAR

Allow your mind to go into "free flow" – that is, let your imagination work radiantly. You won't need to fabricate links: just allow them to pop into your head. When you have made your links, compare them with mine below.

I throw a piece of rolled-up paper at a window. The window opens to reveal a snail. The snail is driving a car. In the back seat of the car is a guitar. This method mixes reality with a little fantasy. It doesn't matter how my mind decided on these ideas. The important point is that they were my first thoughts and they have ensured I will remember those five objects in the correct order.

sticky *magnet*. The magnet pulls itself and you toward a book, which happens to be an *atlas*. Now the four objects are memorable because you have forged a set of links between them all.

EXERCISE 2: Extending the Link Method

I suspect a list of five objects is too easy for you, so why not see how far you can stretch your memory by attempting to recall this list of 20 items. Allow yourself five minutes to form a chain of links between these words, and then see how many items you can recall in sequence before making a mistake:

*DUNGEON   LIZARD   TELEPHONE   TOOTHPASTE
TRUCK   COMPUTER   FLOWERS   SPIDER   CHAIR
DICTIONARY   GARDEN HOSE   CURTAIN   BASKET
CATAPULT   BALLOON   PLUMBER   VOLCANO
TABLE   PORTRAIT   SKI*

Your imagination probably took you on an epic journey, leading you from a dungeon via a truck transporting a computer, then somehow to a catapult that fires at a balloon, and so on through to the final item on the list – a ski.

Score *One point for each item you remembered in sequence.*
Maximum points: 20   Untrained: 4+   Improver: 8+   Master: 18+
If you scored 14 or more, then you have created a highly effective chain of links.

---

08   **Location: the Second Key**

Location is the second key to a perfect memory – locations make up the map of memory. They act as mental filing cabinets, providing a natural and efficient means of storing and retrieving memories. This is because we live in a three-dimensional world where objects can be located – physically or mentally – by where they reside or by following a set of predetermined co-ordinates.

Location was first used as a memory tool more than 2,000 years ago. The ancient Greeks and later the Romans discovered that the best way to remember things was to impose order on them. They did this by choosing a series of places or loci which were already familiar to them. This could consist of rooms around the house, balconies, arches, statues, and so on. Images of what they wanted to recall would then be placed – or rather imagined – at these various *loci*.

Location brings order to our lives and without it our lives would be in chaos. Imagine you were instructed to write down everything you have done today, in order. Like me, you would probably start by retracing your steps and you would most likely use the places you have travelled through to act as a reference.

In Step 6 we learned that it is possible to find a connection between any two sets of information. Likewise, it is possible for your brain to find an association between any word, object, notion or thought, and a location. Take the word "seven": at first glance it is just a number, but once you allow your mind to radiate freely, the word can direct you to a host of associated places: seventh heaven, the cottage from *Snow White and the Seven Dwarves*, a school you attended when you were seven years old, and so on.

Location, then, is an indispensable building-block of memory training, because it lends itself well to association. I use it in a number of my memorization techniques. It is the main feature of the Journey Method – a technique we shall learn in Step 10 and use repeatedly throughout this book.

EXERCISE: Where Do These Words Take You?

Take a look at the following list of 10 words. What places are evoked in your mind by each of these words? Perhaps the word jump reminds you of a river you used to jump over. Catch hold of these places as they pop into your head and jot down as many of them as you can in your notebook. The aim of this exercise is simply to extend your powers of association by demonstrating that any word can trigger a specific associated place in your mind:

| JUMP | SIXTEEN | ELEPHANT | KISS | LADDER |
| FATHER | CLOCK | AUGUST | HOTEL | STORM |

09 **Imagination: the Third Key**

"I am enough of an artist to draw freely upon my imagination.
Imagination is more important than knowledge. Knowledge is limited.
Imagination encircles the world."

ALBERT EINSTEIN (1879–1955)

If association and location are the engine and map of memory respectively, then imagination is the fuel of memory. Imagination is not just the faculty for forming mental images: it is the full creative power of the mind. It is not just the preserve of artists, musicians or poets but a resource that we all have readily available.

Imagination is associated with Theta brainwave activity which is normally at its most active when we are dreaming. However, young children, particularly babies, produce a constant supply of this frequency during waking hours, which may explain why their imaginations often run rampant. The lines between the real and the imagined are blurred, as a teddy bear becomes a living companion and a plastic toy develops magical powers.

As we take on the responsibilities and expectations of adulthood, imagination that was once allowed free range is curbed. I believe there is a direct correlation between the amount of stimulation a person is given as a child and the degree of resistance they show to new ideas in adulthood.

Throughout this book you will be exercising your imagination in a variety of ways, and the more you exercise it the easier it will become to generate memory-building images, ideas and thoughts, and with steadily increasing clarity and speed. As your imagination becomes livelier, so will your memory become stronger: all that's required from you is to allow it to come out to play.

For now, try the following exercise to help you limber up and stretch the boundaries of your imagination.

EXERCISE: Stretching Your Imagination

We are often required to remember information that is, by its nature, inherently uninteresting or unremarkable, such as a list of chores for the day. However, if we use our imagination to embellish an image of the particular item we wish to remember, then we can make it exciting and thus memorable.

Imagine that you need to remember to post an important letter. First, picture a realistic image of an envelope. Then transform this image to make it more memorable. Picture yourself staggering along the road carrying a gigantic envelope. The envelope is decorated with bright blue stars. Now let's add a couple more oddities. Imagine that it smells of chocolate and is ticking like a clock. Now you have created a vivid visual image, and you have added the dimensions of smell and sound. Appealing to two more senses, on top of the visual, makes the item even more memorable in your mind.

---

10 **The Journey Method**

It's now time to put together the three keys of memory – association, location and imagination – by incorporating them into what I believe is the most powerful and complete technique for memorizing any list of information. You will be using all the skills you have already learned: in particular, association (Step 6) and the Link Method (Step 7). I developed this method primarily to help me break world records, and it has been the central weapon in helping me to beat my competitors. I call it the Journey Method, and I believe it will be instrumental in transforming your memory.

Start by choosing a location that is familiar to you, such as your home, your place of work, your home town or a nearby park. The idea is to use this location to prepare a short journey consisting of a series of places or stops along the way. The places are then used to mentally store the items on the list you wish to memorize. The route you take will preserve the original order of the list.

After a while you should find, like me, that you have a favourite journey that you can adopt to memorize almost any type of information for everyday use. In other words, you won't have to prepare a new journey every time you need to apply this technique: you can simply wipe clean your existing, favourite journey and use it again and again to store the fresh set of information that you wish to memorize.

However, if you want to memorize information for long-term storage, or different sets of information in the shorter term, you will need more than one journey. For example, when I am preparing for record attempts or memory competitions, then I require multiple journeys. As we apply the Journey Method throughout this book

I will give you examples of different routes so that you can practise using different journeys. It also helps if your chosen location is relevant to the particular set of data you wish to memorize. For example, I might choose to store sporting statistics along a journey to my local leisure complex.

Your home is probably the most familiar location to you. So let's use the layout of a typical house to demonstrate how to memorize a simple "to do" list of 10 jobs for the day. Choose a route through your own home consisting of 10 stops.

Let's use the following 10 areas as stops on your journey:

1	**FRONT DOOR**	6	**STAIRWAY**
2	**HALLWAY**	7	**MASTER BEDROOM**
3	**KITCHEN**	8	**BATHROOM**
4	**LIVING ROOM**	9	**SPARE BEDROOM**
5	**UTILITY ROOM**	10	**ATTIC**

Make sure that the order of stops forms a logical route through your own home – for example, you would be unlikely to travel from your front door to your attic before visiting the kitchen. You want the route to act as a "guide rope", leading you effortlessly through all the stops in their correct order.

I find when preparing my own routes that it helps to close my eyes and imagine that I am floating through each room as I try to picture all the familiar pieces of furniture, ornaments and personal belongings. As I do this, I count off each place on my fingers until I have reached the final stopping place.

Make a mental note of the halfway stage of your route. For example, I would choose the utility room, or fifth stop, as my halfway point in the above example.

Once you have prepared your journey and know all the stopping points effortlessly forward and backward, then you are ready to start placing items from the list along your route.

Don't consciously try to memorize the items on the list. This is not a test of memory but a demonstration of imagination and association combined with location.

We'll use the following 10 jobs as an example:			
1	CALL VET	6	BUY POSTAGE STAMPS
2	MEND SUNGLASSES	7	COLLECT DRY CLEANING
3	BAKE CUP CAKES	8	CHECK OIL IN CAR
4	VISIT BANK MANAGER	9	PAY WATER BILL
5	BUY BIRTHDAY PRESENT	10	CHANGE LIGHT BULB

All you need to do is form a mental picture of each job and see them at the stops along the route. You can use a number of tools to aid your imagination, such as exaggeration, colour, humour and movement. As well as using all five senses of sight, sound, smell, taste and touch, you will also be using plenty of left-brain logic to complement the sometimes bizarre images formed by the right brain. Create the scene, fix it in your mind, then move on to the next stage.

STOP 1 – Front Door

Position yourself at the front door inside your own home. The first item on your "to do" list is call vet. Imagine opening your front door to find a telephone ringing loudly on your door step. Perhaps your cat is sitting on top of the hand set.

STOP 2 – Hallway

Now position yourself in the hallway before looking at the second task – mend sunglasses. Perhaps the hallway lights are so bright that you quickly reach for some sunglasses to protect your eyes. Or maybe the hallway wallpaper is decorated with a repeat pattern of sunglasses.

STOP 3 – Kitchen

In the kitchen you see rows and rows of *cup cakes* neatly lined up on your work top. An aroma of fresh baking fills the kitchen. There are some more cakes still baking in the oven – which you must rescue before they burn.

STOP 4 – Living Room

Moving into the living room you notice that your bank manager, dressed in a pinstriped suit, is sitting in one of your armchairs sorting through paperwork in preparation for your meeting. There are more papers scattered over the living room floor. Create the scene in your mind's eye.

STOP 5 – Utility Room

You open the door to the Utility Room to find a gigantic present sitting on top of your fresh pile of laundry. Picture the paper it's wrapped in – is it brightly coloured, patterned, shiny, adorned with a bow, and so on? Remember to make a mental note that this is the fifth stage of the journey: picture a bold number 5 painted on the door of the utility room.

Now it's your turn: for the remaining five stops on the journey, listed in the box below, make your own associations to connect these final five jobs to their relevant locations. Remember, at each stage: create a scene, visualize it and add vivid details to make it more memorable.

Stop	Job
STAIRWAY	▶ **BUY POSTAGE STAMPS**
MASTER BEDROOM	▶ **COLLECT DRY CLEANING**
BATHROOM	▶ **CHECK OIL IN CAR**
SPARE BEDROOM	▶ **PAY WATER BILL**
ATTIC	▶ **CHANGE LIGHT BULB**

TEST: The Journey Method

If you have been using the three keys of memory (association, location and imagination), you should now be able to recall many, if not all, of the 10 jobs on your "to do" list. Jot down in your notebook as many jobs as you can recall in their correct order.

Score *Five points for each correctly ordered job – keep a note of your score.*

If you know your route well enough, you won't confuse the order of the list. You could even recite the list in reverse order. All you have to do is walk backward through your journey. And if you want to pinpoint any of the tasks, all that's required is to dip into the journey at a specific stage. If you made a mental note of the fifth stage, you can easily pinpoint the fourth item in the list: it has to be the item one stage before the fifth. How many of these questions can you answer correctly? Again, write down the answers in your notebook.

1   *What task follows cake baking?*
2   *Which job comes before checking oil?*
3   *What is the second job on the list?*
4   *Which task is between buy birthday present and collect dry cleaning?*
5   *At what number on the list is pay water bill?*

Score *10 points for each correct answer.*

Total score *Add up your total points to get your overall score for this exercise.*
Maximum points: 100   Untrained: 25+   Improver: 40+   Master: 85+

11 **Concentration**

We all have days when we find it difficult to concentrate: we may feel under pressure or unduly tired. Other days we are highly productive, alert, full of energy and in control. You've probably heard the expression, "in the Zone", which is sometimes used to describe the mental state of high-performance sportsmen and women – for example, when a tennis player is annihilating his or her opponent in a Grand Slam final. So what exactly is this Zone, and shouldn't all of us have access to it?

Over recent years much of my work has involved measuring the different frequencies of electrical activity produced by the brain using an EEG (electroencephalogram). There are a number of frequencies that we all produce, ranging from slow Delta waves, associated with relaxation, stress control and sleep, to fast Beta waves, associated with increased mental activity, decision making and problem solving. These different frequencies all have their functions and play positive roles in our lives. For example, producing Beta waves enables us to tackle the practical, day-to-day side of life, but if we produced only these waves all the time we would have no time to regenerate, dream or remember efficiently.

Having measured my own brainwaves I noticed that I produce a combination of Alpha and Theta waves – that is, mid-range frequencies – when I'm learning, memorizing and recalling most efficiently. I believe you can train your brain to produce these types of frequencies by regularly exercising your memory.

TIPS: Accessing Your Own Memory Zone

These tips will help you to create the ideal conditions for being "in the Zone":

- Try to find a little time every day to stretch your memory by setting yourself small challenges such as memorizing a list of words, a random sequence of numbers, or maybe some more practical data such as the names of people you have recently come into contact with, either at work or socially. You can use the exercises in this book as practice – repeat them as often as you like, or use them as templates for devising new exercises.

- Before you try to start memorizing or recalling information, make sure you are physically relaxed and seated comfortably in a quiet room free from noise and visual distraction. If you prefer to work with some sound in the background, then try listening to medium-tempo classical music – avoid more frenetic music such as jazz or heavy metal. Remember, you are seeking a mid-range of frequencies between slow and fast brainwaves.

- Slow down your mind by closing your eyes and conjuring up pleasant scenes, such as a favourite holiday location or tranquil times from your past. This will help the production of Alpha and Theta waves.

- When recalling or reviewing data you have memorized, experiment with closing your eyes to help increase the power of Theta, the memory wave.

- Take regular physical exercise to relax and feed your brain with oxygen.

12   The Language of Numbers

How good are you at remembering numbers? Perhaps you have a knack for recalling telephone numbers. Maybe you can remember Personal Identification Numbers (PINs) but birthdays and anniversaries let you down.

We seem to be ever more surrounded by numbers and increasingly we are expected to memorize them in the form of PINs and codes for credit-card security or for accessing special accounts on the internet, or entry codes to offices. Numbers are ubiquitous: telephone numbers, train timetables, weights and measures, bank statements, population statistics, election results ... Wouldn't it be great if we could file away all these numbers for instant and reliable retrieval on demand?

I do not have an innate talent for remembering numbers, but I do have a trained memory which allows me to memorize a sequence of up to 2,000 digits within one hour. How is this possible?

I give numbers a special code which translates them into meaningful, memorable images. This is what I refer to as the language of numbers.

Later on in this book I shall reveal my more advanced number memorization technique – the Dominic System, which is an extremely efficient method for memorizing multiple-digit numbers. However, the simpler Number-Shape System is a great way to store a sequence of digits from telephone numbers and four-digit PINs to calendar and historical dates, and much more.

THE NUMBER-SHAPE SYSTEM

The Number-Shape System works by translating a single-digit number into an image resembling its shape. For example, the number 8 with a small stretch of the imagination has the shape of a snowman. So, to remember that oxygen has the atomic number 8, picture a snowman wearing an oxygen mask.

The number 6 could resemble an elephant's trunk. The number 7 has the shape of a boomerang. To remind you that you have a number 67 bus to catch, imagine an elephant standing at the bus stop throwing a boomerang with its trunk: a somewhat unlikely scene but certainly one you won't forget. Now, suddenly, numbers come to life. They become animated, take on a unique significance and are instantly more memorable.

Let's look at another example. How would you memorize the four-digit PIN 1580? Perhaps this is a PIN for a cash dispenser, in which case you could stage the scene at your local bank. Imagine walking into your bank carrying a gigantic pencil (a number shape for 1) – perhaps you are about to draft a business plan. Inside the bank there is a seahorse (a number shape for 5) queuing up at the cash desk. Behind the window is a snowman (a number shape for 8) bouncing a soccer ball (a number shape for 0) on his head. Run through this scene in your mind a few times and you shouldn't forget the PIN in a hurry.

TOOLS: A Pictorial Vocabulary

What shapes do single-digit numbers evoke for you? 0 a ball; 9 a balloon on a string? Take a look at the examples here. Either memorize these equivalents or make up your own.

0 = BALL, RING
OR WHEEL

I = PENCIL, CANDLE
OR ROCKET

2 = SWAN OR
SNAKE

4 = FLAG ON A FLAG POLE
OR SAIL ON A BOAT

3 = PAIR OF LIPS
OR HANDCUFFS

5 = SEAHORSE OR
S-SHAPED HOOK

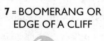

7 = BOOMERANG OR
EDGE OF A CLIFF

6 = ELEPHANT'S TRUNK
OR GOLF CLUB

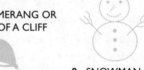

8 = SNOWMAN OR
EGG-TIMER

9 = MONOCLE OR
BALLOON ON A STRING

EXERCISE: Number-Shape Memorization

You may have noticed that in the examples I gave on page 41, I connected number shapes together using the Link Method from Step 7. To remind you, the Link Method works by connecting one object to the next by creating some form of artificial, imagined common ground between the two items.

Try to memorize the following 20-digit number using the Number-Shape System. Convert each number into its equivalent shape (use either your own number shapes or mine) and connect them together using the Link Method. So to start, I imagine throwing a boomerang at a balloon on a string. Now you continue by connecting the balloon on a string to a ball, and so on.

7 9 0 4 6 2 1 3 5 8 5 9 9 4 0 1 3 2 7 6

You should now have created a story involving a chain of 20 linked number shapes starting with a boomerang or a cliff edge and ending with an elephant's trunk or a golf club. Now try to write down the sequence of numbers in your notebook.

Score *One point for each digit you can recall before making a mistake.*

Maximum points: 20   Untrained: 4+   Improver: 8+   Master: 18+

13   The Number-Rhyme System

An alternative to Number Shapes is the Number-Rhyme System. This involves forming the key image for a number by a word that rhymes with it. For example, *door* could be used to rhyme with the number *four*. A door then becomes the key image for that number and can be used to help you memorize any information involving the number four.

Let's say you want to remember that you are taking a flight from Terminal 4 at an international airport. You could imagine carrying a door with you as you arrive at the airport. This simple, quick thought will ensure you will arrive at the correct terminal.

How could you remember to buy two pounds of apples? Well, *shoe* rhymes with the number *two*. So you could picture yourself in your local grocery store carrying apples in a large shoe.

What words would you choose to rhyme with the numbers one, three, or eight? Here are some suggestions for all 10 digits. Either memorize their equivalent rhymes or create your own:

Numbers and Their Rhyme Words:

0 = HERO	**5 = HIVE, CHIVE or DIVE**
1 = GUN, BUN or SUN	**6 = STICKS or BRICKS**
2 = SHOE, GLUE or SUE	**7 = HEAVEN or KEVIN**
3 = TREE, BEE or KEY	**8 = GATE, BAIT or WEIGHT**
4 = DOOR, SORE or BOAR	**9 = WINE, SIGN or PINE**

EXERCISE: Number Rhymes

Use Number Rhymes to memorize the following items of trivia:

1 *The world population is approximately six billion*
2 *The average brain comprises two percent of a person's body weight*
3 *There are seven Australian states*
4 *An ant has five noses*
5 *Queen Victoria of England had nine children*
6 *A newborn camel has zero humps*
7 *There are four planets larger than Earth*
8 *There are three Great Pyramids at Giza*

Now, cover up the top half of this page and see how many answers you can give to the following questions – jot down your answers in your notebook:

1 *How many humps does a newborn camel have?*
2 *What is the world population to the nearest billion?*
3 *How many noses does an ant have?*
4 *How many planets are there larger than Earth?*
5 *How many Australian states are there?*
6 *How many children did Queen Victoria of England have?*
7 *How many Great Pyramids are there at Giza?*
8 *What percentage of body weight can be accounted for by the brain?*

Score *10 points for each correct answer.*
Maximum points: 80   Untrained: 40+   Improver: 60+   Master: 80

14   The Alphabet System

I was once required to memorize the NATO phonetic alphabet for a job. To do this I used the Journey Method described in Step 10. The journey is a highly effective memory tool, allowing information to be absorbed rapidly in the form of symbolic images along a pre-planned route. However, after I started using this alphabet I no longer needed to use the journey to recall the words as the information soon became fixed in my long-term memory.

The phonetic alphabet is a useful memory device in itself. Any data I need to memorize involving single letters I automatically substitute with their symbolic equivalents. So, to remember a random code of three letters, *Z G H*, I picture a *Zulu* hitting a *Golf* ball at a *Hotel*. It's also a useful alternative to the Journey Method as it provides a storage facility for memorizing a list of up to 26 pieces of information such as 26 great composers, artists or poets.

Here is a list of the phonetic alphabet:			
ALPHA	*HOTEL*	*OSCAR*	*VICTOR*
BRAVO	*INDIA*	*PAPA*	*WHISKEY*
CHARLIE	*JULIET*	*QUEBEC*	*X-RAY*
DELTA	*KILO*	*ROMEO*	*YANKEE*
ECHO	*LIMA*	*SIERRA*	*ZULU*
FOXTROT	*MIKE*	*TANGO*	
GOLF	*NOVEMBER*	*UNIFORM*	

EXERCISE: Using The Alphabet System

In order to memorize the phonetic alphabet in the first place, use the Journey Method (Step 10) to devise a route consisting of 26 stages. Plant the image you create for each letter along each stage of your route. Perhaps an alpha male orangutan is at the first stage, an opera tenor to whom an audience is shouting Bravo is placed at the second stage, and so on, until a *Zulu* warrior finishes the route at stage 26.

Keep reviewing the journey until you know all 26 letters in their symbolic forms, backward and forward through the alphabet. Each image needs to be so ingrained that it instantly comes to mind, and you do not need to scan through the journey to recall the phonetic letter and its associated image.

Now, use the Link Method (Step 7) to memorize the following sequence of 10 letters by linking the images you have created and already memorized for the Alphabet System. Write down the letters in your notebook.

P   N   U   S   J   M   E   V   M   S

Score *10 points for each letter you can recall in sequence before making a mistake.*
Maximum points: 100   Untrained: 30+   Improver: 60+   Master: 90+

You now know the order of the planets starting with the furthest from the Sun:

**PLUTO   NEPTUNE   URANUS   SATURN   JUPITER
MARS   EARTH   VENUS   MERCURY   SUN**

chapter 2

Memory Construction

In chapter 1 you evaluated the performance of your untrained memory. You also learned about the key principles and skills involved in training your memory: these are the basic tools in your memory tool box.

In this chapter we are going to practise using those tools – Association, Imagination, the Link Method, the Journey Method, and so forth – by applying them to the memorization of all sorts of different information, such as word spellings (Step 17) and the capital cities of the world (Step 18). You will soon see just how versatile and adaptable these techniques are, and how useful you will find them in many day-to-day situations – for example, when you need to put names to faces (Step 15), remember directions when you have stopped to ask the way (Step 16), or call to mind a joke whenever you want to amuse your friends (Step 24).

I shall also be introducing you to some new techniques, such as the Dominic System (Step 23). This is my own method for remembering longer sequences of numbers by associating all the two-digit numbers from 00 to 99 with a character. Don't worry, you will start with just the first 20 digits from 00 to 19. The exercises and tests along the way will show you how much your memory is improving with every step.

15 **How to Remember Names and Faces**

"Forgive your enemies, but never forget their names."

JOHN F. KENNEDY (1917–63)

Of all the concerns that people have shared with me about their memory, putting names to faces is number one on the list. As humans we have an inbuilt mechanism for recognizing faces (this is probably an evolutionary hangover from the time when we needed to discern our friends from our enemies). If remembering a face presents no difficulty, then why is it that so many of us have a problem when it comes to remembering names? There's a very simple answer: our names do not *describe* our faces.

My first name is Dominic, but this does not help to portray my face to you. And the matter is not made easier by the fact that

I share my surname – O'Brien – with tens of thousands of others around the world. Imagine trying to memorize one hundred people in a room whose names were just Bob, Mary, Michael or Jane.

GIVE A FACE A PLACE

What are the most effective ways of ensuring you never experience that embarrassing moment at a party, which we've all suffered at some time, when you are forced to ask, "Sorry, what was your name again?" 30 seconds after being introduced to someone? The most important thing is to recognize that we tend to associate a person with a particular place. Think of a time when you have bumped into someone in the street whose face is very familiar but whose name escapes you. What is the first thing you do to try to recall who this person is? You ask yourself, "Where do I know this person from?"

It is the place that will release most of the memories connected with this person including, hopefully, his or her name.

One trick I use to memorize people for the first time is to designate a place for each of them. I do this by imagining where I might expect to find this person. Let's say you are being introduced to a lady at a party and for some reason you think that she looks like a librarian. Perhaps she has a studious air about her. Now you have prepared a location for her. You are told that her name is "Margaret". Now think of someone that you know of called Margaret (a relative, friend, actress, politician, or whoever) and picture her at your local library. The first Margaret you think of is the ex British Prime Minister, Margaret Thatcher – so you imagine her working at the library. The next time you see this lady's face you will be able to retrace her name in the following way:

FACE ⇨ LIBRARY ⇨ THATCHER SCENE ⇨ MARGARET

This may seem like a lengthy process to connect the face to the name, but remember that your brain recalls information in a flash as long as there is chain of associated connections for it to travel along.

FOCUS ON FACIAL FEATURES

If I meet someone whose features are particularly striking, instead of associating that person with a place, I sometimes find it is easier to connect their name directly to their physical appearance. For example, you are introduced to a man called Peter Byrd and immediately you connect his name with his face as he has a rather hooked nose (a bit like a bird's beak). Your brain can now make more connections and quickly seizes on "Pet", short for Peter, and there you have your link: Pet Bird.

I find the best way to tackle a complicated surname is to break it down into syllables and then turn these syllables into images. Names, like numbers, need to be translated into images so that our brains can digest them. Our brains thrive on making connections, so when we are confronted with a name that doesn't represent a face, then the answer is to forge an artificial link between the two.

The following exercise will give you a chance to try out your brain's agility in making links. You can use any of the techniques described in this step: that is, place a person in a familiar location, or identify physical resemblances, or distinctive characteristics of a name or face to make associations and form memorable images. For example, how might you commit Maria Hutton to memory? The surname "Hutton" sounds to me like "hat on", so I picture Maria Hutton wearing a hat, with her braids poking out. I notice that she has rosy cheeks, so I imagine she is flushed from singing the line "I've just met a girl named Maria" from the musical, *West Side Story*. This will remind me of her first name.

EXERCISE: Matching Names to Faces

Study the following 10 faces and try to form links to their names:

MARIA HUTTON	PETER JARVIS	ALAN WAKEFIELD	JANE FRENCH	PAULA TULIP
STEVE PALMER	ALISON CLARK	IAN PATE	BOB SAXTON	ROWENA WARD

Now cover these faces and look at the same 10 faces in a different sequence below and try to match the correct names to the faces.

Score *Five points for each correct first name and five points for each correct surname.*

Maximum points: 100   Untrained: 20+   Improver: 50+   Master: 80+

16   **How to Remember Directions**

Does the following predicament sound familiar to you? You are in an unfamiliar area and you're late for an appointment. You stop to ask a passer-by for directions, and will have to rely on your memory, as you do not have a pen and paper to hand. The passer-by bombards you with a sequence of directions that you know you are going to forget unless you hear them repeated several times. But you don't have time for this, and you decide to take a chance that you will remember the directions to get you to your destination. Of course, it is likely that you'll need to stop again a couple of miles down the street and ask someone else for further directions.

However, by applying a simple memory technique you need only listen to a set of directions once. Let's imagine you are lost in an American town and a sympathetic stranger gives you the following set of directions:

	Example of a Set of Directions:
I	**TAKE THE SECOND LEFT INTO KING STREET**
2	**AT THE GARDEN CENTER TURN LEFT INTO FINSBURY STREET**
3	**AT THE END OF THIS BLOCK TURN RIGHT**
4	**FOLLOW THE STREET SIGNS TO THE ART GALLERY**
5	**AT THE SECOND SET OF STOP LIGHTS TURN LEFT**
6	**AT THE "NEEDLES RESTAURANT" TURN LEFT INTO RAM'S COURT**
7	**LOOK FOR THE RED BUILDING, NUMBER EIGHT**

At first glance this may appear to be too much information to absorb all in one go. However, if you have been working through the exercises in this book so far, you should already be feeling confident about your progress, particularly when it comes to memorizing a sequence of just seven pieces of information.

This is how I tackle memorizing directions: I regard them as a sequence of shopping items, say, and I use the Journey Method to store them quickly. Naturally, you need to have your journey pre-prepared.

As there are seven individual directions, you need a short journey of just seven stages, which you can use to store the information. For example, you could use a favourite vacation destination as your backdrop for the journey.

	Example of a Journey through a Familiar Vacation Location:
1	**HOTEL ENTRANCE**
2	**LOBBY**
3	**ELEVATORS**
4	**RESTAURANT RECEPTION**
5	**TABLE BY THE WINDOW**
6	**BALCONY**
7	**SWIMMING POOL**

EXERCISE: Remembering Directions

Once you have prepared your seven-stage journey, as described on pages 54–5, you are ready to memorize the directions.

Remember to always position yourself at the first stage of your journey before you start to memorize the instructions. Let's take a look at how I would see the first few stages of the journey. In this case, I start by picturing myself at the entrance to the hotel:

FIRST STAGE
Hotel entrance

FIRST DIRECTION
Take the second left into King Street

There are no hard and fast rules as to what method you use to translate numbers and words into pictures. However, I tend to use Number Shapes (see Step 12) whenever a single-digit number is involved, as in "second left". So, to the left of the hotel entrance, I picture a swan (number shape for 2) flying over a startled king.

SECOND STAGE
Lobby

SECOND DIRECTION
At the Garden Center turn left into Finsbury Street

The hotel lobby is furnished with an array of dramatic plants and flowers. To the left of the reception area I imagine a shark's fin poking out of one of the plants. All that's required here is an image to trigger the name of the street. A shark's fin should be enough to remember the name Finsbury without having to concern myself with the second syllable, -bury.

THIRD STAGE
Elevators

THIRD DIRECTION
At the end of this block turn right

To remember to turn right I picture myself taking the righthand elevator.

FOURTH STAGE
Restaurant reception

FOURTH DIRECTION
Follow the street signs to the art gallery

At the restaurant front desk I imagine the headwaiter admiring a collection of oil paintings hanging on the wall above the desk.

FIFTH STAGE
Table by the window

FIFTH DIRECTION
At the second set of stop lights turn left

I picture a set of stop lights in the middle of the table. A swan flies over the top of the lights and out of the open window on the left.

Now over to you. Continue creating connections between the remaining two journey stages and two sets of directions, perhaps finishing with a scene that connects the swimming pool with the Number Shape for 8: a snowman. Quickly review your journey to make sure you have all seven scenes fixed in your head, then see if you can write down the directions in your notebook.

Score *10 points for each correct direction before a wrong turn is made.*

Maximum points: 70   Untrained: 20+   Improver: 40+   Master: 60+

17   How to Remember Spellings

Whenever I am forced to think twice about how to spell a commonly misspelt word, I tend to rely on a mnemonic strategy that I used to rectify misspelling when I was first confronted with the dilemma. For example, I know I will never confuse the correct spelling of the word *separate* with its commonly misspelled counterpart, *seperate*, because I think of a *para*-trooper landing in the middle of the word separating the two halves: *se para te*.

EXERCISE: Identifying Correct Spellings of Words

As a tease, here is a selection of some of the most commonly misspelt words. The correct and incorrect versions are scattered between both columns. Can you identify the correctly spelt words?

ACCIDENTLY	ACCIDENTALLY
ACCOMMODATE	ACCOMODATE
CEMETARY	CEMETERY
DEFINITELY	DEFINATELY
ECSTASY	ECSTACY
EMBARRASS	EMBARASS
HANDKERCHIEF	HANKERCHIEF
INDEPENDANT	INDEPENDENT
MOMENTO	MEMENTO
SUPERCEDE	SUPERSEDE

Check the correct spellings listed below to see how many words you recognized correctly.

SUPERSEDE	ECSTASY
MEMENTO	DEFINITELY
INDEPENDENT	CEMETERY
HANDKERCHIEF	ACCOMMODATE
EMBARRASS	ACCIDENTALLY

Score 10 points for each word that you recognized correctly.

Maximum points: 100   Untrained: 10+   Improver: 50+   Master: 100

The trick is to look out for connections between certain patterns of letters and the meanings of the words. Then use visualization and association to make those connections memorable. For example, notice the symmetry of the three Es in the word c E m E t E ry. They stick out like gravestones. I put my *hand* in my pocket to pull out my *hand*kerchief. I use my *memory* to remind me that a *memento*, not a *momento*, is a reminder.

The mechanism on which memory works and thrives is association. Somewhere, in any word you care to think of, there is a link to be forged between the spelling and the meaning of a word.

If you didn't fair too well on your first attempt at that list of

10 words, then read through them again, this time spotting any little connection that will ensure you get the spelling right.

18 How to Remember Countries and Their Capitals

In Steps 3 and 4 we looked at the use of mnemonics as an aid to help us remember anything from the colours of the spectrum to the order of the nine planets. (Can you still remember them?) And so it follows that mnemonics can be used to memorize a whole array of geographical facts. If I had been introduced to the world of mnemonics when I was at school, I might have found the whole process of learning much more enjoyable.

If only my geography teacher had pointed out that one way to remember that Canberra is the capital of Australia is to look at the shape of the country. Australia is shaped somewhat like a camera, which helps me to remember its capital, Canberra.

If my teacher had said that the way to remember the difference between the Arctic and Antarctic was to think of looking up at an *arch* and down at an *ant*, then I might have found their geographical positions less confusing.

Mnemonics are a great way to remove the drudgery of learning by rote as they provide chains of links between pieces of information that can easily be retraced and therefore recalled at a later date. It's almost as if short-term memory is bypassed as the data gets transferred straight into long-term memory where it is cemented with vivid, symbolic, associated imagery.

EXERCISE: Countries and Capitals

Take a look at the following pairs of lists and, using imagination and visualization, try to make a link between each country and its capital. I have deliberately avoided the more familiar countries to make this exercise more of a challenge.

For example, to remember that Tallinn is the capital of Estonia I picture a lady I know called Esther walking into an Inn with a tall entrance. When I see the word Estonia again I will be reminded of Esther, which will lead me to the tall Inn and the capital, Tallinn. Remember, all you require is a trigger to help you to recall the data. The images you choose do not have to be exact matches.

COUNTRY	CAPITAL
ANGOLA	*LUANDA*
THE BAHAMAS	*NASSAU*
BULGARIA	*SOFIA*
COSTA RICA	*SAN JOSÉ*
ESTONIA	*TALLINN*
FIJI	*SUVA*
MOROCCO	*RABAT*
OMAN	*MUSCAT*
QATAR	*DOHA*
ZAMBIA	*LUSAKA*

exercise continued

Now find out how well you made those links by answering the following questions in your notebook:

1   *What is the capital of Fiji?*

2   *Lusaka is the capital of which country?*

3   *What is the capital of The Bahamas?*

4   *What is the capital of Qatar?*

5   *Tallinn is the capital of which country?*

6   *Muscat is the capital of which country?*

7   *What is the capital of Angola?*

8   *San José is the capital of which country?*

9   *What is the capital of Bulgaria?*

10   *Rabat is the capital of which country?*

Score *10 points for each correct answer.*
Maximum points: 100   Untrained: 30+   Improver: 60+   Master: 80+

A typical score for someone who has read through these geographical facts just once without using any memory devices would be around 30 points. The information would need to be read over and over again before a perfect score could be achieved. However, the little time you spent in creating associations between these countries and their capitals should have enabled you to absorb the information much more effectively, resulting in a higher score. If you scored more than 60 points, then your memory is shaping up very well indeed.

19   **Learning a Foreign Language**

Whether you need to learn another language for business or travel, want to help your children study a second language, or just want basic conversational skills in another language, this step reveals how it is possible to learn foreign words at a rapid pace.

The key is to create an image by finding a common link between the sound of a foreign word and its meaning in your own language. For example, bacon is Speck in German. To make a link, picture a slice of bacon with an unsavoury-looking speck on it.

To make this method even more effective we need a place to store these images for instant retrieval. In many languages, we will also need to know the gender of each noun. My Gender Zones method enables us to perform both these functions simultaneously.

Gender Zones

In languages with two genders such as Spanish or French, Gender Zones provide two discrete geographical regions in your mind where everything is either masculine or feminine. For example, any French word that is masculine I would place in my home county of Surrey, England. Any feminine word I would place in another county, Cornwall. Both regions must be familiar to you to make this method work. For example, by fixing my mind on a certain hospital in Surrey, I know that hospital in French is masculine, *un hôpital*. To remember that post office is a feminine word, *la poste*, I think of a specific post office in Cornwall. Once I remind myself of these places I will never confuse the gender of the two words.

These Gender Zones also act as filing systems for storing your linked images. For example, the French for sea is *mer*, which sounds to me like "mayor". I picture a mayor in full regalia swimming in the sea off the coast of Cornwall, and now I have performed two tasks in one image. I know that sea is *mer*, and feminine, because I have placed the image in Cornwall (my feminine zone).

EXERCISE: Gender Zones

Try learning the following 10 Spanish words and their genders. Use the three keys of memory – association, location and imagination. Choose your own Gender Zones, then process each word in the following way:

1 *Look at the gender of the word and place it in the correct zone.*

2 *Find a link between the sound of the Spanish word and its meaning.*

3 *Create an image or scene and place it strategically in a precise part of the chosen zone.*

So, when I look at the first word in the list opposite, I know I have to think of a place in Cornwall (my feminine zone) connected with salt. I think of a friend of mine, Sally or Sal, dispensing salt over a plate of fish and chips at a little café I know well in Cornwall. Now you work through the rest of the words on the list:

ENGLISH	SPANISH	GENDER (M/F)
Salt	*La sal*	*(f)*
Foot	*El pie*	*(m)*
Field	*El campo*	*(m)*
Sleeve	*La manga*	*(f)*
Cat	*El gato*	*(m)*
Cot	*La cuna*	*(f)*
Oar	*El remo*	*(m)*
Wall	*El muro*	*(m)*
Star	*La estrella*	*(f)*
Bed	*La cama*	*(f)*

Now copy down the 10 English words in your notebook. Then cover this page and see if you can write down the Spanish equivalent and its correct gender alongside each of the English nouns.

Score *Five points for each correct word and five for each gender.*

Maximum points: 100   Untrained: 30+   Improver: 60+   Master: 90+

Once you have established your Gender Zones to store all your nouns, there is nothing to stop you from designating other areas that are familiar to you for adjectives, verbs, numbers, months, and so on. For example, the most commonly used adjectives could be stored in your local park. Action verbs such as to run, to walk, to jump, to swim, and so on could all be stored at your local sports complex. Use exactly the same techniques you have employed in the exercise above to create these new zones and their word links.

20 **How to Remember Your Past**

How far back in your past can you remember? Very few people can remember anything of the first year of their life, and most can remember only from the age of three or four onward. Thus, the few memories that we have of our childhood are very precious to us.

We attach great significance to these first memories, setting each one as some kind of milestone in our early life. Whatever it is that has fixed them in our minds, these memories play a major role in shaping us – they are part of who we are.

One method I use to return to memories from the past is what I call "Time Travel". The idea is to return to a location from your past, which will trigger a series of memories. The location could be a school, a relative's house, or a village you once lived in.

In the following exercise you can try out this method for yourself. Your aim is to return to a particular location and time in your past, so that you can release and enrich your memories.

This is a beneficial exercise for the memory in itself, and you may decide to spend five or 10 minutes a day working on a specific place and time from your past. You should notice that each time you return to the scene you will be starting with a clearer overview of that time gone by. As your associations with that particular place and time strengthen, you will find that one memory will trigger another. You may also find that memories will pop into your dreams, and pieces of the mental jigsaw puzzle that were once lost may now be restored.

EXERCISE: Time Travel

This exercise gives you the oppotunity to try out the Time Travel method for yourself. Remember to use those three keys of memory – association, location and imagination – to conjure up the scene from the past and bring it to life.

1   Choose a specific starting point such as a school playground, a museum, an old attic or a special part of your garden where you frequently spent time. Wherever you start, try to picture little details in your mind's eye: maybe a painting on a wall, a glass cabinet containing a book you once read, or whatever.

2   Try to recall people connected with this place: their voices, the way they laughed, certain mannerisms.

3   Try to recapture the sounds you once heard in this place, such as a squeaky door, a train that used to pass by, children playing outside, or the music you listened to at that time. What smells do you associate with this place? Fresh flowers? Polished wood? Try to recall how your surroundings felt to touch, such as a stone wall or iron gate, or the fabric covering the arm of an old chair.

4   Try to remember your emotional state at that specific time. Were you generally happy, melancholy, care-free, unsure of the world, in love? The more layers you can tap into from your past, the more memories will be released.

21 **How to Remember the Elements**

A few years ago I made a television commercial in Florida on the subject of memory. I was asked to illustrate the power of my techniques by training two school children, aged around 11 years old, to memorize the first 30 elements of the Periodic Table.

Neither child had been taught any memory techniques before, and yet after about 20 minutes both children were able to recite the correct order of the elements backward and forward, and if they were asked, for example, "What is the atomic number of Phosphorus?" they were able to give the correct answer, "15".

To teach the children how to memorize the elements, I took them on a short journey around the television studios, stopping at suitable places where I asked them to imagine the different elements coming to life.

We started at the front gates of the studios where they imagined a small explosion taking place. This would help them to remember the first element, Hydrogen. We continued along our route, stopping at each stage to make an association. At the fourth stop, they couldn't think of an association for Beryllium (the fourth element), so instead I asked them to picture a little old lady named Beryl doing some knitting in the editing suite (the fourth stop). At the tenth stop (the recording studio), they pictured a flashing neon sign above the door, and so on. By the end of our journey we had converted all 30 elements into meaningful scenes which were easily recalled, and the journey preserved the order of this list.

EXERCISE: The Periodic Table

Here is a list of the first 15 elements of the Periodic Table:

ATOMIC NUMBER	ELEMENT
1	*Hydrogen*
2	*Helium*
3	*Lithium*
4	*Beryllium*
5	*Boron*
6	*Carbon*
7	*Nitrogen*
8	*Oxygen*
9	*Fluorine*
10	*Neon*
11	*Sodium*
12	*Magnesium*
13	*Aluminium*
14	*Silicon*
15	*Phosphorus*

Using your own journey, prepare a route of 15 stops and use it to memorize the first 15 elements. By now you should be able to do this in about eight minutes. Then write down the 15 elements in order in your notebook.

Score *10 points for each element you can recall before making a mistake.*
Maximum points: 150   Untrained: 50+   Improver: 90+   Master: 140+

22   **Develop Your Declarative Memory**

In this step we are going to look at how developing our "declarative" or conscious memory can speed up our ability to absorb new information. Let's say you wish to learn a new sport or discipline, such as tennis or yoga. You will spend the first lesson converting what your instructor, DVD or workbook is telling you into physical actions. The conscious effort you make to memorize the order of these instructions is known as declarative memory.

In time, your actions become automatic and there is no longer any conscious act of recall. But memory still plays its part – the kind known as reflexive memory (learning by repetition). However, wouldn't it be easier if your declarative memory was able to absorb and recall all these commands in an instant? Think how much sooner you could acquire this new skill if you could learn every piece of advice accurately.

The Journey Method can radically improve the efficiency of your declarative memory. It gives you the best possible start if you are learning a new discipline, especially one that involves many moves to make in sequence. In the exercise opposite I am going to show you how a sequence of yoga moves can be stored quickly into long-term memory using a short journey. By initially performing each posture in a different room or area of your home you will implant the physical memory of each posture as well as fix the order of the moves in your mind. So when you come to practise the sequence as a whole, your journey will remind you of the order.

EXERCISE: Simplified Yoga Poses

These five poses are adapted from the Kneeling-Cat-Swan yoga pose:

1   Kneel down with your hands on your thighs, eyes closed.

2   As you breathe in, gently lift your arms overhead and come up to a raised kneeling position.

3   As you breathe out, gently bring your hands to the floor so you are kneeling on all fours.

4   Inhale, bend your elbows and lift the centre of your chest forward and upward. (This is the Cat pose.)

5   As you breathe out, push your bottom back so you are sitting on your heels. Leave your arms stretched out in front of you. (This is the Swan pose.)

Plan a five-stage journey around your home so that you can store each posture at a different stage along the route. For example, you might store the first posture in your hallway, the second one in your living room, and so on.

Position yourself physically at your first stage and perform the first posture. Then move on to your second stage and perform the second pose, and so on. Later, see if you can practise the complete sequence as a fluid series of movements by mentally running through your five-stage journey.

23 **The Dominic System I**

In Steps 12 and 13 we looked at simple systems to translate numbers into pictures using Number Shapes and Number Rhymes. These mnemonic devices are a great introduction to learning what I call the "language" of numbers, and I use them for memorizing anything involving a single-digit number.

However, when I began memorizing much larger numbers for competitions I realized that I needed a method that would allow me to recognize numbers instantly as pictures, to the point where I could read through and make sense of a sequence of 100 digits, say, in much the same way as I am able to read through and understand a sentence composed of 100 letters grouped into words.

Thus the Dominic System was born. Dominic stands for: Decipherment Of Mnemonically Interpreted Numbers Into Characters. This system is more complex than Number Shapes or Number Rhymes. However, if you invest a little time in learning it, you will find it a much more efficient method of converting numbers into symbolic images.

With the Dominic System any two-digit number (and of course, there are 100 of them from 00 to 99) can be translated into a person. Why turn numbers into people? For the simple reason that people, especially ones who are familiar to me and vivid in character, are so much easier to remember than numbers. Why not choose objects instead of people? Because I find people are more flexible than objects. They can be imagined in almost any situation and they react in countless ways to different environments. Throw a custard pie at a chair and not much happens, but throw one at a person and you are bound to get a response.

HOW DOES IT WORK?

To start with, in your notebook, write the 100 numbers from 00 to 99 in a column. You will need three more columns: Letters/Person/Action and Prop (see page 75 for reference). You will see why in a moment. Then take a look at any of these numbers that may have significance for you. For example, 10 instantly makes me think of a British Prime Minister because that's where he or she lives, at 10 Downing Street. Perhaps 49 triggers a player from the "49ers" American Superbowl team.

When I see 57 I automatically think of my Godfather because I was born in 1957. It doesn't matter how you get there as long as the number always leads you to that particular person.

Once you have exhausted this line of investigation, then the next step is to assign letters to the remaining two-digit numbers (the ones which you can't immediately convert into people). To do this you will need to assign all the digits to letters of the alphabet, following a standard set of conversions. Here is the set I use:

| 1=A | 2=B | 3=C | 4=D | 5=E | 6=S | 7=G | 8=H | 9=N | 0=O |

Numbers 1 to 5 and 7 and 8 are paired with the letters that match their positions in the alphabet. O represents zero because they look the same. S is paired with six because six has a strong "S" sound. N represents 9 because the word nine contains two "N"s.

Once you have learnt this simple sequence, numbers can be paired together to form the initials of various people. These might include friends, relatives, politicians, comedians, actors, sportsmen and women, even infamous villains.

Let's see how this might work. Take any two-digit combination, such as 72. By translating this number into its equivalent letters from the Dominic Alphabet you get GB (7=G, 2=B). Who can you think of that has the initials GB? George Bush perhaps? George Bush now becomes your key image, or rather, key person, for the number 72. The number 40 translates into DO (4=D, 0=O), which just happens to be my own initials.

It is not necessary for you to conjure up a perfect photographic image of these people, you just need to recognize them for what they represent. The best way to do this is to assign an action and prop to each person. George Bush's action and prop combination is waving the American flag. Dominic O'Brien's action and prop combination is dealing out playing cards.

Now all of a sudden numbers become meaningful. We have breathed life into them and they begin to take on a personality of their own.

In the advanced section of this book I will be showing you how you can use the Dominic System to memorize groups of four or more numbers by combining the characters. But before we get to that stage it's a good idea to start with the first few combinations of two-digit numbers to get a feel for how this system works.

Here are the combinations of the numbers from 00 to 09:

NUMBER	LETTERS	PERSON	ACTION AND PROP
00	OO	Olive Oyl	Opening can of spinach
01	OA	Oswald Avery	Looking down a microscope
02	OB	Orlando Bloom	Wearing elf ears
03	OC	Oliver Cromwell	Loading musket
04	OD	Officer Dibble	Chasing Top Cat
05	OE	Old Etonian	Wearing boater hat
06	OS	Oliver Stone	Sitting in his Director's chair
07	OG	Organ Grinder	Holding monkey
08	OH	Oliver Hardy	Wearing bowler hat
09	ON	Oliver North	Swearing an oath

I have suggested a name, action and prop for each set of initials. Either transfer my examples to the list in your notebook or create your own characters, and commit each one to memory.

Now move on to the next 10 numbers (10 to 19). Again, use the characters I have suggested or think up your own.

NUMBER	LETTERS	PERSON	ACTION AND PROP
10	AO	Annie Oakley	Firing a gun
11	AA	Andre Agassi	Swinging a tennis racquet
12	AB	Anne Boleyn	Being beheaded
13	AC	Al Capone	Carrying bottle of liquor
14	AD	Artful Dodger	Picking a pocket
15	AE	Albert Einstein	Chalking a chalkboard
16	AS	Arnold Schwarzenegger	Flexing his muscles
17	AG	Alec Guinness	Wielding a lightsaber
18	AH	Adolf Hitler	Goose-stepping
19	AN	Alfred Nobel	Lighting dynamite

The Dominic System is a key memory method which we will primarily use in conjunction with the Journey Method. I will introduce you to the Dominic System gradually, at a pace designed in relation to this 52-step course. And as I do so, I encourage you to take the time and effort to learn each set of initials which will eventually give you a relatively simple language of 100 people. This system will ensure that ultimately you end up with an amazingly efficient facility for memorizing numerical information.

EXERCISE: Using the Dominic System I

If you have learned the first 20 people in the Dominic System (see pages 75–6), you should now be able to memorize the following random sequence of 20 digits using the Journey Method (Step 10).

1 8 1 1 0 6 0 7 0 0 1 8 1 7 1 2 0 3 0 8

Your route need consist of only 10 stages. Create a journey – for example, around your garden – and see each two-digit number as a person planted at each stage of the journey. This is how the numbers translate into letters:

18	11	06	07	00	18	17	12	03	08
AH	AA	OS	OG	OO	AH	AG	AB	OC	OH

Using the three keys of imagination, association and location, work your way through the sequence starting with the person represented by 18. I would picture Adolf Hitler (AH=18) goose-stepping by the rose bed. Next is Andre Agassi (AA=11) playing tennis by the shed. And so on ... until at the far end of my garden is Oliver Hardy (OH=08), one of the silent-movie comedy duo Laurel and Hardy, wearing a bowler hat.

Write the numbers down in your notebook. How many numbers can you recall in sequence before a mistake is made?

Score *Five points for each correctly remembered digit before you make your first error.*

Maximum points: 100   Untrained: 30+   Improver: 60+   Master: 80+

24 **How to Remember Jokes**

Why is it that we so often struggle to remember jokes? Well, when we listen to jokes we are usually so busy enjoying them that we don't give a moment's thought to committing them to memory.

Summarizing a joke visually, either by translating it into a scene or by linking it imaginatively with an appropriate image, is one way to fix it more firmly in our minds. In theory, we have only to recall the image and the joke will spring back to life – assuming that it's a memorable joke in the first place. But how can we be sure of recollecting our visual trigger? Imagine you find yourself chatting with a friend about the circus, and deep in the back of your mind lies a joke about a lion tamer. You attempted, many months ago, to commit this joke to memory by linking it with a vivid image of the lion tamer swallowed by the lion – a fate which only just escapes him in the joke itself. But because you have forgotten that you once heard and tried to memorize this joke, your friend's references to circuses are not enough to trigger the memory of the image. And so you miss the opportunity to amuse.

What, then, can we do to ensure that the joke we once memorized springs to mind exactly when we want it? The answer is that we must consciously build a repertoire of jokes and rehearse them from time to time until they all become second nature to us. Whatever memory technique is used thus becomes a kind of scaffolding: it is useful for the preparatory stage – building the repertoire – but can be discarded once the whole body of jokes is well established in our mind. To build your repertoire, use the Journey Method (see Step 10). Say your house or apartment has 10 rooms; you might add to this a friend's house or apartment to give you 20 rooms, or 20 positions, in your overall journey. Attach an image to each new joke that you learn, and place each image mentally in the next room you come to, going around the houses in your pre-determined sequence.

Tell five different people each new joke, soon after you have heard it: this also helps to fix the memory. And from time to time rehearse your whole repertoire of 20 jokes once you have filled both houses. In time these jokes will become as familiar to you as the alphabet, and you will be able to summon up any of them whenever the occasion arises.

Anecdotal and Word-based Jokes

Jokes often take the form of mini stories, in which case a single vivid image may not be enough to remember them by. The solution might be to attach an image to each separate episode *within* the joke, then imaginatively link each image to a particular feature within the room to which you have assigned the joke as a whole. Further guidelines are given in Step 25, on how to remember fiction. Many jokes, of course, depend heavily on word play, and you might decide that you will need to put extra effort into memorizing key phrases – in which case consider the advice given for Step 40, on memorizing poetry.

25 How to Remember Fiction

Reading novels is a great pastime for vacations. Our various commitments can make it hard to grab more than half an hour or so at a time, and then perhaps not more than two or three times per week. So it's easy to forget the beginning of the book before you are half-way through. Plot connections can pass you by. You may fail to understand motivation that has been set up many pages back. You may completely miss the point of one or more sub-plots, even if the main plot is well within your grasp.

"No, I can follow even complex plots pretty well," you may protest. But how long do you keep all but the most rudimentary details in your head afterwards? A month or two? Six months? If for so little time, that's a pity because you are missing out on the retrospective enjoyment to be gained from your reading. Using memory discipline will make your reading something you can appreciate in retrospect as well as in the present.

Few people would want to go to the trouble of learning a novel by the Journey Method, but there's no reason why you shouldn't develop a Mind Map (Step 28) to help you get your bearings. The most useful technique, though, is to invest the book with imaginative energy. Picture the scenes and encounters as vividly as you can. Try to empathize with characters' predicaments. To help you imagine a particular figure in terms of their appearance, personality or life circumstances, summon up someone you know who fits, or almost fits, the bill. Use places you know to help you visualize the settings, if this helps. Or if the location is exotic, borrow from what you have seen in magazines or on the television.

Where many readers go astray is in imagining that a novel is to be experienced only for as long as you're reading it. In fact, your recall will be better if you let the characters and their situations live for a while in your head after you have put the book down. Imagine what it *feels* like to be a character in this book.

EXERCISE: Remembering a Complete Movie

Movies are like novels: it's easy to forget even the good ones after a few months – and when particular films come up in conversation you may kick yourself for not being able to remember what you liked, or disliked, about them. Of course, some movies – particularly ones involving crime detection – deliberately tease with false plot trails. Flashbacks can also be confusing. After seeing a movie like this, it's fun to go out with friends and try to reconstruct the twists of the plot from beginning to end. You might even do this competitively, each person scoring points for the details they can recall. The main characters' names should be easy enough if you've really concentrated (you'd be surprised how many people come out of a movie without having absorbed this basic data); but see if you can recall minor characters as well, and place names, and the way people's homes were furnished. In fact, the scope for memory testing is limitless.

26 **Read Faster and Remember More**

We live in an age of information. There simply isn't enough time in the day to read every word in every piece of media presented to us. The good news is that we don't need to read every single word on a page to understand its content. In fact, by focusing on key words, you can comprehend and store the information just as efficiently as you would if you read the text word for word, thus speeding up your reading. So, you could say that speed reading is a speed memorization technique.

THE PRINCIPLES OF SPEED READING
The average reading speed is a little more than 200 words per minute for the average student with varying rates of comprehension. However, this speed can be increased – in excess of 1,000 words per minute with practice – by following these inextricably linked keys of speed reading:

Use a pointer. Although it may seem unnatural to begin with, using some form of pointer, such as a pen or your finger, helps the eye glide smoothly along the line. This allows you to develop a continuous rhythm, without distraction. Read a whole passage – or a short article – without breaking off, reading each sentence only once and taking in only the essentials.

If you give your full attention, you will not need to back-track: minor words need not detain you. Keep up a smooth, steady pace, and try increasing the speed with which you move the pointer.

EXERCISE: Speed Reading

This exercise lets you experiment with the technique of speed reading. First you need to calculate your existing reading speed, then monitor yourself as you work at improving it.

1   Take any piece of continuous prose in a book, magazine or newspaper and read, in your usual way, as much text as would fill one page in this book – about 250 words. Use a stopwatch to time yourself; or ask a friend to keep time for you in seconds and indicate to them as soon as you reach the end of your passage. Then calculate your reading speed using this formula:

(Total words read ÷ Time taken in seconds) x 60 = Words per minute

2   Check your level of comprehension by jotting down in your notebook the main points you have absorbed from your reading, including all facts and examples. Or get your friend to ask you comprehension questions. Satisfy yourself that you have absorbed the essentials of the passage.

3   Take another passage of similar length and similar density of content. This time, apply the speed reading principles described opposite.

4   Calculate your new reading speed using the formula above. Check your comprehension as before. Compare your second result with your first.

5   Experiment with different speeds of reading on different passages until you find a workable balance of speed and comprehension.

27 **How to Remember Quotations**

To be able to slip into your ordinary conversation a quote from a writer such as Oscar Wilde or Mark Twain or a thinker such as Albert Einstein or Ralph Waldo Emerson is a sure way to impress or to give you the advantage in a debate. But quotations are so slippery! And there's no point in half-remembering a quotation, or giving up half-way through or not remembering who said it, as that's certain to undermine the impression you want to give of being on nodding terms with the great and good – at least through their writings. In this step we look at ways in which useful or inspiring quotations can be memorized for long-term retention.

As with jokes, the best way to fix a quote in your memory is to associate it with a vivid image. But there are two differences to bear in mind. First, with quotations you need to be able to recall the text verbatim (although with foreign quotations there will usually be some leeway over the translation). And second, you will need to remember who it was who wrote or uttered the remark in the first place.

You may find that the best way to store quotes is to build a repertoire of them using the Journey Method, following the advice given for remembering jokes (Step 24). As we're dealing with the written word, a book store or local library makes an ideal location for your journey – you could even place each quote in the relevant department within the building. If you can, devise an image that fuses the author of the quote with its content, and store this in the appropriate stage of your journey, as part of your quotation repertoire. Further aspects might be memorized to help you to reconstruct the particular phraseology of the quote.

Now let's take an example, and see how you might approach it. The following quote is from Sir Winston Churchill:

"A pessimist sees the difficulty in every opportunity; an optimist sees the opportunity in every difficulty."

The first step is to find a key image which summarizes the essence of the quote. Now the classic image in this quote is the glass that the optimist would describe as half-full, the pessimist as half-empty. So you picture Churchill – rotund and enjoying a cigar – holding a half-full glass (of Scotch perhaps) with an optimistic expression on his face. The "Win" of Winston links with optimism and further reinforces the message. You might notice that the two opposing views are a mirror image of each other ("the difficulty in every opportunity ... the opportunity in every difficulty"), and imagine Churchill reflected in the mirror-like surface of the glass.

If you are unfamiliar with the author of the quote, and thus have to remember a name that is devoid of associations for you, you might break the surname down into syllables and memorize one or more of these, using your own imagination in following any of the associational links I have previously described in this book.

EXERCISE: Remembering Quotations

Take a look at the following three quotes. Try to memorize them by convenient imagery (use any of the techniques described on pages 84–5). Devise an image for the source of each quote, too. Obviously, different people are going to have different degrees of familiarity with the names. A sports enthusiast will only need to remember "Jor-" (jaw?) for Michael Jordan's name to roll out, while someone who has no interest in sport may need a more elaborate cue, for the first name (the archangel?) as well as the second (the river in the Holy Land?).

Post your images in convenient places using the Journey Method – perhaps the first three rooms of your house or apartment. We are testing only short-term memory here, so the aim is to see if you can remember, 30 minutes from now, all three quotes plus the Churchill quote on page 85. Set an alarm clock.

"I can accept failure. Everybody fails sometimes. But I can't accept not trying."

MICHAEL JORDAN, AMERICAN BASKETBALL STAR

"If I have seen further, it is by standing on the shoulders of giants."

SIR ISAAC NEWTON, HISTORIC SCIENTIST

"Judge a man by his questions rather than by his answers."

VOLTAIRE, FRENCH THINKER OF THE 18TH CENTURY

Scoring *10 points for each correctly remembered quote (you must be word-perfect to score) and five points for each correct name.*

Maximum points: 60   Untrained: 20+   Improver: 30+   Master: 50+

28   **Memory and Mind Maps®**

Mind Mapping offers a simplified diagrammatic overview of a subject and is an ideal way to present information in a visual form that your brain can easily grasp. It is a useful technique for recording a summary of what you have read in a book, newspaper or magazine or heard in a lecture or in a TV or radio program.

Mind-Maps® were invented in the 1960s by my friend and colleague, Tony Buzan. Tony saw Mind Maps as a way of utilizing the left and right hemispheres of the brain simultaneously, in cooperation with each other. The analytical, logical left brain understands and assesses the information; while the imaginative, intuitive right brain finds a visual form in which to present it. Below is a summary of the different processes associated with each hemisphere, to help you understand how Mind Mapping works.

Left Hemisphere	Right Hemisphere
Speech	*Creativity*
Analysis	*Colour perception*
Sequencing	*Spatial awareness*
Logic	*Creating an overview*
Linear thinking	*Day-dreaming*
Rational thinking	*Intuition*
Numbers and word recognition	*Face and object recognition*

A Mind Map is a good way to represent the relative importance of different topics – and to appraise them or remind yourself of them at a glance. The central themes are clearly defined and all extraneous information is eliminated. You can see the whole picture and the key details all at the same time.

A SAMPLE MIND MAP ON GLOBAL WARMING

This simplified Mind Map shows one possible approach. Classic Mind Mapping would have more pictures and would attempt to use single words rather than phrases wherever possible. Also, each branch would be in a different colour.

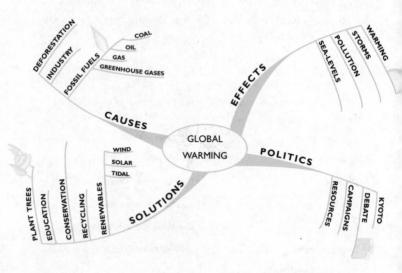

Exercise: Making Your Own Mind Map

Take a sheet of paper and some coloured pens or pencils. (Use ink for the lettering and coloured pencils for the graphics.) You might decide to start with a rough sketch so that you can adjust the proportions a little once you have everything mapped out initially on paper.

The point of this exercise is to create and memorize two Mind Maps on:

1   Some topic on which you wish to become better informed. You can choose any field – perhaps an aspect of sport or music, or some episode in history, or something more technical such as the way a car engine works. You might already know the key facts and want to build up a clearer picture. Do some background reading, making draft Mind Maps as you proceed: do not take any longhand notes, and restrict yourself to the key points, expressed in as few words as possible. Add organically to the Mind Map as you gain more knowledge by further reading. When you feel that you have read and understood enough, prepare your final Mind Map, in colour, with suitable imagery and graphics. Commit it to memory. After two or three days see if you can reproduce it from memory alone.

2   The key priorities in your life, in relation to such questions as home, money, relationships, work, leisure, skills, values, ambitions, travel, and so on. You can use this kind of Mind Map as a way to determine how you see yourself progressing in the future. Add simple pictures to help fix the things that matter most to you. If you wish, as with the first Mind Map, the sizing of these images can be used to reflect their relative importance.

So how would you go about Mind Mapping, say, a lecture? The speaker might follow an eccentric order of presentation – he or she might start with a minor point to grab your attention and build up slowly to the main point, or state it first, followed by a series of qualifications. As you construct your Mind Map you need to be flexible enough to accommodate such shifts of emphasis. You may not know what the key points are until the lecture is over.

Many people will choose to do a draft in pen or pencil before producing a finalized version in colour. By creating simple graphic images within the Mind Map (don't worry, no artistic expertise is required), you help to make key points vivid and memorable. And by using different colours of ink or pencil, you can emphasize the different strands of subject matter to help you "read" the Mind Map more speedily or more effectively – which makes the device an excellent revision tool. It is also a useful way to prepare an essay, to reduce a manual, workbook or article to a simpler, clearer form, or to clarify your ideas about any kind of project.

When you choose to commit a Mind Map to memory, the spatial aspects help you to cement the contents there. The idea is to absorb and recall the whole map, as you would recall a place you know, or a map of where you live. Let's say you want to remember the effects of global warming. Picture the branch at the top right-hand side of the map, and read off, in your memory, the key words positioned there. Any pictorial symbol you have placed alongside will further help you with the process of recollection.

29 How to Remember Speeches and Presentations

For some people the thought of standing up in front of even a small audience and saying a few words can be highly intimidating. The best presentations or speeches are well prepared and delivered from memory, the speaker maintaining roving eye contact with the audience. But nerves can undermine the pleasure of giving or hearing such speeches, not least because stage fright is a notorious memory thief: confronting an expectant audience, even the best-rehearsed of speechmakers may suddenly find that their mind has gone completely blank. Panic!

USING A MIND MAP

One of the most effective ways to prepare a speech or presentation is to get all your ideas down onto a Mind Map, as described in the previous step. You then fix this set of cues in your mind and proceed in a logical order through the diagram – for example, clockwise, starting at upper left, or whatever seems the most natural order to you. The key images and/or words that you plot on your map become prompts for whatever you want to say. By the time you give your speech, the map will be thoroughly familiar to you. Even while you were devising it in the first place, it will have started to imprint itself in your mind; and then you will have reinforced the memory every time you studied it subsequently. Of course, just before it's time for you to make the speech it's wise to steal a few moments at least to have a final look – and, if there is time, rehearse the stages of the speech in your head using the Mind Map itself to check afterwards that you haven't omitted any of your points.

The beauty of using a Mind Map to prepare a speech is that it will give you confidence. You know that literally you have the whole speech mapped out in your mind in a familiar image, and that you can travel around your image at will. Confidence is self-reinforcing. Just knowing that you are well equipped helps you to do a good job; and this in turn increases your confidence even more next time you are faced with a similar challenge.

Of course, in many speechmaking situations no one would be surprised or disappointed if you held a crib-sheet in your hand and glanced at it from time to time whenever you needed a prompt. Holding a single sheet with your Mind Map on it is certainly going to give a better impression than sheaves of notes which you have to rifle through to find your place.

USING THE JOURNEY METHOD

Another way to prepare a note-free delivery is to write down the key words of your speech and convert them by association to memorable images which you then place at different stages along a chosen route using the Journey Method (see Step 10). You might opt to use your own house or apartment, or the walk from your home to the train station. Further guidance on using this technique is given with an example, opposite.

TIPS: Speechmaking with Key Points and Phrases

To try to remember a speech word for word, like an actor learning a script, is an objective fraught with pitfalls. The problem is that once you've embarked on recalling your text verbatim, if for some reason (such as nerves) you forget the next sentence, you can find yourself completely at a loss. That's why it's better to memorize your speech in terms of essential points – what you want to say, without reference to how you plan to say it.

To fix these points in your memory, you can use imaginative associations to convert them into images which you mentally position in a sequence of locations following the Journey Method (see Step 10). You then recapture these images, and thus your points, by repeating the journey. For example, if at the end of your speech you plan to thank the farmer whose field you've borrowed for the summer fair, you might decide to place a smelly cow in your guest bedroom (maybe in bed dirtying the sheets) or a gigantic hog at the train station (maybe trying to squeeze into a carriage).

At times in your speech you may need to refer to names or numbers. You have already learned how to commit names and numbers to memory in Steps 15, 12, 13 and 23, so follow the guidelines given for these steps.

In speeches designed to amuse or give pleasure, rather than be purely informative, the telling phrase is a powerful tool. It is easy enough to combine the Journey Method with learning by heart a few eloquent sentences. Having composed a particularly well-polished sentence or sequence of sentences, you may decide to spin off from one of the key words (ideally one that comes early on) an image that you can place on your memory journey, so that the whole sentence or sequence rolls out as soon as that image has been prompted again. Practise your best phrases plenty of times, to facilitate this effect.

30 The Art of Revision and Maximizing Recall

So far in this book we have looked at various mnemonic techniques for memorizing a range of information including PINs, short shopping lists, directions, foreign vocabulary, quotations and short speeches. Most of these techniques involve the three keys of association, location and imagination. In particular, using the Journey Method, based on familiar locations, appears to bridge the gap between short- and long-term retention. It's as though the data bypasses short-term memory, allowing more information to go straight into the long-term memory bank. These memory techniques remove the drudgery of traditional methods of rote learning, which in comparison can be slow, repetitive and less efficient. But to ensure that information remains in your long-term memory, it's essential to know when and how often to review it.

EBBINGHAUS AND THE RECALL CURVE

One of the first people to carry out experiments on human memory was the German philosopher Hermann Ebbinghaus (1850–1909). He devised a way of testing memory using a series of nonsense syllables – seemingly meaningless, unmemorable syllables, for example: DAJ. He would read through a list of 20 such items several times until he was able to memorize the exact sequence. He then measured his retention of the list after varying time periods. This was probably the first ever formal learning curve. Ebbinghaus observed that, for a series of information, data near the beginning and end of the list was easier to recall than that in the middle. These tendencies are known as the Primacy and Recency effects respectively, and a U-shaped curve graphically illustrated the findings.

Ebbinghaus also discovered that the best way to maintain maximum recall was to review data regularly until what he called "overlearning" had been achieved.

To consolidate your memory of stored data you need to know when to review it. Here is my suggested schedule of review times, which I find works extremely well for most types of material:

FIRST REVIEW	▶	*IMMEDIATELY*
SECOND REVIEW	▶	*24 HOURS LATER*
THIRD REVIEW	▶	*ONE WEEK LATER*
FOURTH REVIEW	▶	*ONE MONTH LATER*
FIFTH REVIEW	▶	*THREE MONTHS LATER*

You can follow this "rule of five" with some of the exercises in this book. The exercise itself will provide the first review stage. You can then return to it after the suggested time periods and re-test yourself to ensure that the data remains in your long-term memory.

Memory Power

This chapter comprises the more advanced steps of my memory program. Some of these steps will involve practising key techniques you are already familiar with, but at a more advanced level. For example, you will progress to creating a journey of 52 stages. And some steps, such as How to Remember Telephone Conversations (Step 32) and How to Remember the News (Step 38), require you to combine a number of these techniques, including the Journey Method, Remembering Names, Directions, Countries and Capitals, and Quotations, as well as the Dominic System, to memorize a wide range of data.

You will continue learning the Dominic System (for the numbers 20 to 99) in Steps 31 and 33 to complete your repertoire of 100 characters. We will develop this system to include complex images, enabling you to memorize important dates and complicated sequences of numbers with ease.

In other steps I shall be introducing you to new techniques, such as my specially-devised coding system to help you to commit to memory any date in the last few centuries. I shall also be teaching you how to memorize a deck of playing cards (something that's got me banned from the casinos of Las Vegas!). The exercises will monitor your progress along the way.

31 **The Dominic System II**

In Step 23 I introduced you to the Dominic System for learning a new language: the language of numbers. I asked you to draw up a list of the first 20 numbers from 00 to 19, then, by using a carefully devised code, translate them into letters which formed the initials of various people. Each person also had a prop and/or an action. For example, the number 06 translates into Oliver Stone (0 = O, 6=S), whose action is sitting in his director's chair. If you think you need to recap the Dominic System method, then refer to Step 23.

Assuming you are now fluent in recognizing the first 20 pairs of numbers as people, take a look at the next group of two-digit numbers and see which initials they produce.

Turn to the list you drew up in your notebook for the Dominic System in Step 23 and fill in the numbers, letters, people and actions/props for the numbers 20 to 39. I have given you suggestions in the box opposite. These are the characters that work best for me, but everyone has their own frames of reference, influenced by their culture, nationality, age, tastes, experiences and so forth. So don't worry if you are unfamiliar with any of the people I have used. Use your own associations to come up with an alternative name, action and prop for that particular set of initials. Remember, you can use a mixture of famous people, and people known to you personally, such as friends or relatives. Once you have committed these 20 characters to memory, try the exercise on page 100.

NUMBER	LETTERS	PERSON	ACTION AND PROP
20	BO	Billy Ocean	Holding a microphone
21	BA	Bryan Adams	Shooting a bow and arrow
22	BB	Brigitte Bardot	Pouting into a compact mirror
23	BC	Bill Clinton	Waving the American flag
24	BD	Bette Davis	Wearing a satin evening gown
25	BE	Bill Evans	Playing a piano
26	BS	Bart Simpson	Skateboarding
27	BG	Billy Graham	Preaching from a podium
28	BH	Buddy Holly	Wearing his trademark glasses
29	BN	Brigitte Nielsen	Wearing boxing gloves
30	CO	Chris O'Donnell	Dressed as Robin
31	CA	Charlie's Angels	Flicking their hair
32	CB	Charlie Brown	Playing with Snoopy
33	CC	Charlie Chaplin	Swishing a cane
34	CD	Celine Dion	Sitting on an iceberg
35	CE	Clint Eastwood	Wearing a poncho
36	CS	Claudia Schiffer	Striding along a catwalk
37	CG	Che Guevara	Holding a machine gun
38	CH	Charlton Heston	Riding a chariot
39	CN	Chuck Norris	Doing a karate kick

EXERCISE: Using the Dominic System II

You should now be able to memorize the following random sequence of 20 digits using the Dominic System and the Journey Method.

3 6 3 3 2 0 3 8 2 9 3 1 2 4 2 2 3 7 2 5

As in the exercise in Step 23, create a short journey consisting of 10 stages and see each two-digit number as a person planted along each stage of the journey. To remind you, this is how the numbers convert into letters:

36	33	20	38	29	31	24	22	37	25
CS	CC	BO	CH	BN	CA	BD	BB	CG	BE

As you travel along your route, you meet each person represented by each pair of initials, performing his or her action. So you might imagine Claudia Schiffer (CS = 36) at the first stage of your journey, striding along a catwalk, and at the second stage Charlie Chaplin (CC = 33) is swishing a cane, and so on.

After a quick review of the journey see how many numbers you can recall by writing them down in your notebook.

Score *Five points for each digit you can recall in sequence before making a mistake. Maximum points: 100   Untrained: 30+   Improver: 70+   Master: 90+ Compare this with your previous effort on page 77. Although you are working with a new set of characters, you are now more familiar with the Dominic System, so I would expect you to improve on your earlier score.*

32 **How to Remember Telephone Conversations**

Remembering what you hear is very different from remembering what you read: it is harder to control the inflow of data. However, a telephone conversation is a two-way interaction: you have some measure of control. You can ask the person you're talking to to slow down or repeat information. Likewise, you can repeat information back to them to check you have heard it correctly.

Of course, anyone who is given crucial information over the phone is going to want to write it down if at all possible – your aim may be to hold it in your mind only for as long as it takes for you to locate some paper and something to write with. But thinking of any information as temporary data that you need hold onto only for a minute or two is a sure way to forget it. Using the techniques in this step will prevent this from happening.

The exercise on the following pages gives you training in combining a whole miscellany of different techniques to memorize different types of information at speed.

Telephone conversations often require us to remember numerical data: dates, telephone numbers, quantities, flight details, and so on, as well as names of people and places, and directions. So, in addition to the Journey Method, you are going to be using several other techniques along the way, such as Number Shapes, Number Rhymes, the Dominic System, Remembering Names, and Directions.

EXERCISE: Remembering a Telephone Conversation

In this exercise you will practise combining various techniques at a moment's notice. When using the Journey Method at such short notice I always choose one of several tried and tested routes which I know won't let me down. Ask a friend to help you do this exercise. Your friend will act as your tour operator, who has called to give you the details of a vacation booking. Finally, answer the 10 questions.

1   Select your most tried and tested journey – perhaps a route around your home (see Step 10).

2   Ask your friend to read out the telephone message on the page opposite.

3   As you listen to the spoken message, convert the essential details into key images and position them at each stop along your journey.

Hint: To memorize a single-digit number, I would use the Number-Shape or Number-Rhyme System; to memorize a two-digit number, I would use the Dominic System; to memorize a three-digit number, I would use the Dominic System combined with a Number Shape or Number Rhyme; to memorize a short sequence of letters, I would use the Alphabet System; and to memorize a mixture of letters and numbers, I would use the Alphabet System combined with the Dominic System and a Number Shape or Number Rhyme.

You can practise this exercise as many times as you like – simply ask your friend to change the original details to new ones.

"Hello, I'm calling from Caribbean Tours to give you your vacation details. You are flying from New York to Barbados with Caribbean Premier Airlines (CPA).

You fly from JFK airport, terminal eight – your departure time is 0735hrs. You will arrive at the Grantley Adams International Airport (BGI), terminal one, at 1315hrs. Your flight reference number is CP/45022.

Once you arrive you will need to report to your tour representative, Sally Gardiner, who will be standing to the left of the foreign exchange desk in the arrivals lounge. You will then take the transfer bus to your hotel – the Island Bay Resort. If you require travel insurance, then you will need to pay an additional $38.20. I think that covers everything. Do you have any questions?"

1   *Which airline are you flying with?*

2   *Which airport and terminal will you depart from?*

3   *What is your departure time?*

4   *Which airport and terminal will you arrive at?*

5   *What is your arrival time?*

6   *What is your flight reference number?*

7   *What is the name of your tour representative?*

8   *Where will you find her?*

9   *What is the name of your hotel?*

10 *How much are you required to pay for travel insurance?*

Score *10 points for each correctly answered question.*

Maximum points: 100   Untrained: 20+   Improver: 50+   Master: 80+

33 **The Dominic System III**

If you think you've mastered the Dominic System for the numbers 00–39 (Steps 23 and 31), then it's time to learn the remaining numbers, from 40 to 99, listed below and on pages 105–106.

As in the previous Dominic System steps, look at the numbers and see whose initials you can come up with. Again, add the details to the list in your notebook and once you have a match, decide on an action and prop that suit your particular character.

Remember, your cast of characters can include friends, relatives, politicians, comedians, actors, sportsmen and women, characters from movies, and so on.

NUMBER	LETTERS	PERSON	ACTION AND PROP
40	DO	Dominic O'Brien	Playing cards
41	DA	Douglas Adams	Hitchhiking
42	DB	David Bowie	Dancing in the street
43	DC	David Copperfield	Pulling a rabbit from a hat
44	DD	Donald Duck	Shaking his tail feather
45	DE	Duke Ellington	Conducting music
46	DS	Deion Saunders	Playing American football
47	DG	Dizzy Gillespie	Playing the trumpet
48	DH	Daryl Hannah	Turning into a mermaid
49	DN	David Niven	Flying a hot air balloon
50	EO	Eugene O'Neill	Drinking whisky on the rocks
51	EA	Elizabeth Arden	Spraying perfume

NUMBER	LETTERS	PERSON	ACTION AND PROP
52	EB	Emily Brontë	Writing a novel
53	EC	Eric Clapton	Playing his guitar
54	ED	Eliza Doolittle	Selling flowers
55	EE	Edward Elgar	Composing music
56	ES	Ebenezer Scrooge	Counting money
57	EG	Eric Gill	Sculpting a war memorial
58	EH	Ernest Hemingway	Fishing
59	EN	E. Nesbit	Blowing a whistle
60	SO	Scarlett O'Hara	Fainting
61	SA	Scott of the Antarctic	Trudging through a blizzard
62	SB	Sleeping Beauty	Sleeping
63	SC	Sean Connery	Drinking a martini
64	SD	Salvador Dali	Twirling his moustache
65	SE	Stefan Edberg	Holding up a trophy
66	SS	Steven Spielberg	Pointing, with ET
67	SG	Stéphane Grappelli	Playing a violin
68	SH	Stephen Hawking	Looking through telescope
69	SN	Sam Neill	Running from a dinosaur
70	GO	Gary Oldman	Dressed as Dracula
71	GA	Georgio Armani	Sketching suit designs
72	GB	George Bush	Stroking his dog
73	GC	George Clooney	Wearing a stethoscope
74	GD	Geena Davis	Driving a Thunderbird car
75	GE	George Everest	Climbing with ropes

NUMBER	LETTERS	PERSON	ACTION AND PROP
76	GS	Gilbert and Sullivan	Wearing aprons
77	GG	Greta Garbo	Leaning against a lamppost
78	GH	Gene Hackman	Catching drug dealers
79	GN	Greg Norman	Swinging a golf club
80	HO	Hugh O'Neill	Charging on horseback
81	HA	Hank Aaron	Hitting a home run
82	HB	Humphrey Bogart	Wearing a mac and hat
83	HC	Hillary Clinton	Giving a speech
84	HD	Humphry Davy	Holding a miner's lamp
85	HE	Herb Elliott	Running
86	HS	Homer Simpson	Eating donuts
87	HG	Hugh Grant	Getting married
88	HH	Hulk Hogan	Wrestling
89	HN	Horatio Nelson	Standing at the helm
90	NO	Nick Owen	Sitting on a sofa
91	NA	Neil Armstrong	Wearing a spacesuit
92	NB	Norman Bates	Taking a shower
93	NC	Noel Coward	Smoking a cigarette
94	ND	Neil Diamond	Forever in blue jeans
95	NE	Nelson Eddy	Dressed as a Mountie
96	NS	Nina Simone	Singing at a piano
97	NG	Nell Gwyn	Selling oranges
98	NH	Nathaniel Hawthorne	Wearing a scarlet letter
99	NN	Nicholas Nickleby	Flogging Mr Squeers

Once you have converted this final group of 60 two-digit numbers into people and have committed them to memory, you can attempt the following exercise.

EXERCISE: Using the Dominic System III

Memorize the sequence of 20 digits below, using the Journey Method.

5 3 4 2 7 7 6 8 9 1 8 7 8 2 5 9 6 5 4 0

Remember, first split the sequence into pairs of numbers and translate each two-digit number into a pair of initials. Then create a short journey of 10 stages and see each pair of initials as a person planted along each stage of your journey. Again, this is how the numbers convert into letters:

53	42	77	68	91	87	82	59	65	40
EC	DB	GG	SH	NA	HG	HB	EN	SE	DO

Try to recall the 20-digit sequence and write it down in your notebook.

Score *Five points for each single digit you can recall in sequence before making a mistake.*

Maximum points: 100   Untrained: 30+   Improver: 75+   Master: 95+
Compare your score with your previous efforts in Steps 23 and 31. Again, I would expect you to improve on your previous scores.

34 How to Memorize a Deck of Playing Cards

My inspiration for taking up memory training came from watching international memory master Creighton Carvello on television memorizing a deck of shuffled playing cards in the incredibly fast time of two minutes and 59 seconds. The cards were dealt out one at a time, one on top of the other: in other words, he had just a single sighting of each card. How, then, was it possible for this man to link 52 unconnected pieces of data together in less than three minutes? It was this question that inspired me to take up a deck of cards and try to fathom the answer for myself.

It soon dawned on me that what I needed to do was visualize each of the 52 cards as a particular person. I could then use the Journey Method to preserve the order of the cards.

After three months of intense training not only could I memorize a whole deck in less than three minutes but I was now memorizing multiple decks of cards. Later on I shall be explaining how it is possible to memorize multiple decks. But for now, here is how you too can memorize a single deck of cards.

NUMBER CARDS

You must first assign a person to every card between Ace and 10. We'll deal with the court cards later. Cards can be treated like numbers. The easiest way to assign a person to each card is to translate them into pairs of letters which then represent the initials of names (a technique you have already learned as the Dominic System). The number of the card gives you the first letter. So, taking 1 to be Ace conveniently gives us the letter A. 2 becomes B, 3 becomes C, and so

on. To make things simpler, the 10 becomes O. The suit provides you
with the second letter:

♣	**CLUBS**	=	**C**
♦	**DIAMONDS**	=	**D**
♥	**HEARTS**	=	**H**
♠	**SPADES**	=	**S**

In your notebook, list the 10 cards from 1 (Ace) to 0 (10) in a column.
Make four more columns for the suits: Clubs, Diamonds, Hearts and
Spades. Fill in all the columns by converting each card into a pair
of initials. For example, the Ace of Clubs becomes the initials **AC**;
the **5** of **D**iamonds becomes **ED**; the **8** of **H**earts becomes **HH**; and
the **10** of Spades becomes **OS**. Now fill in the columns using the
people, actions and props from your Dominic System (Steps 23, 31
and 33). The Ace of Clubs is Al Capone (1=A; Clubs=C); the **5** of
Diamonds is Eliza Doolittle (5=E; Diamonds=D); the **8** of **H**earts
is Hulk Hogan (8 = H; Hearts = H); and the **10** of Spades is Oliver
Stone (10 = O; Spades = S).

FACE CARDS

Now we need to deal with the court, or face, cards. Start by looking at the faces of each card: if their faces resemble any people you know, use that particular person to represent the card. If not, then you need to decide on a character for them. I have listed my examples below, based on the associations I make with each suit: Clubs make me think of aggression or golf; Diamonds represent actual diamonds and wealth; Hearts remind me of romantic leads in movies; and Spades (which resemble inverted hearts) represent villains. Make sure each character has their own action or prop.

CARD	SUIT	PERSON	ACTION AND PROP
Jack	Clubs	Tiger Woods	Swinging a golf club
Queen	Clubs	Buffy the Vampire Slayer	Wielding a club
King	Clubs	Mohammad Ali	Wearing boxing gloves
Jack	Diamonds	Prince Harry	Playing polo
Queen	Diamonds	Marilyn Monroe	Dripping with diamonds
King	Diamonds	Bill Gates	Counting his diamonds
Jack	Hearts	Shakespeare's Romeo	Climbing onto a balcony
Queen	Hearts	Grace Kelly	Blowing kisses
King	Hearts	Cary Grant	Tipping his hat
Jack	Spades	Draco Malfoy	Mixing a potion
Queen	Spades	Cruella De Ville	Walking Dalmatians
King	Spades	Darth Vader	Wearing his black helmet

EXERCISE 1: Warm-up

Once you can identify each card as a person, you are ready to start memorizing your first deck of cards. However, I suggest you attempt 10 cards as a warm-up before tackling the whole sequence of 52.

1 Form a mental journey consisting of 10 stages.

2 Deal out 10 playing cards and convert each card into its character. Imagine seeing each character posted along each stage of your journey, performing his or her own action. If the King of Diamonds is your first card, Bill Gates is counting diamonds at the first stage of the journey, and so on.

3 Replay your journey and jot down the order of the cards in your notebook.

Score *10 points for each correctly remembered card before a mistake is made.*
Maximum points: 100   Untrained: 20+   Improver: 40+   Master: 90+

EXERCISE 2: Whole Deck

If you feel ready, you can now try to memorize your first deck of cards. Follow the instructions given in the exercise above, only this time you will need to plan a journey of 52 significant stops and deal out the whole deck of cards. You can monitor your progress by timing yourself. Over the next four weeks aim to memorize a deck in less than 15 minutes. Eventually, with practice, you should be able to break the five-minute barrier.

35 **How to Become a Human Calendar**

If someone mentions to me any date from the last couple of centuries I can tell them which day of the week that date fell on, and in a matter of seconds. For example, if someone says they were married on February 13th 1953, I am able to instantly tell them that day was a Friday. How am I able to do this?

The year, month and day are equal to a set of co-ordinates which lead me to a "place" that reveals the day of the week. As usual I am employing the recurrent theme of the three keys of memory – association, location and imagination – to guide me. It is beyond the scope of this book to explain the mathematics behind these codes, but trust me – they work!

I break a date into its component parts – year, month and day – and I give each part a single-digit code number, between 0 and 6. I then use these numbers to calculate the day of the week for the particular date I am seeking.

THE YEAR CODES

I have devised a coding system for all the years from 1800 to 2099. We shall start with the years 1900 to 1999. First, I choose six rooms in my house. I allocate to each room a number between 0 and 6. As the garden is not a room, I call it zero. Then I place each year in a particular room (see box). To memorize these Year Codes you will be combining location with the Dominic System to imagine each year as a person in a particular room at a big party.

SYSTEM: The Year Codes

BEDROOM: CODE 1
1901, 1907, 1912, 1918, 1929,
1935, 1940, 1946, 1957, 1963,
1968, 1974, 1985, 1991, 1996

KITCHEN: CODE 5
1904, 1910, 1921, 1927, 1932,
1938, 1949, 1955, 1960, 1966,
1977, 1983, 1988, 1994

SPARE ROOM: CODE 2
1902, 1913, 1919, 1924, 1930,
1941, 1947, 1952, 1958, 1969,
1975, 1980, 1986, 1997

STUDY: CODE 6
1905, 1911, 1916, 1922, 1933,
1939, 1944, 1950, 1961, 1967,
1972, 1978, 1989, 1995

BATHROOM: CODE 3
1903, 1908, 1914, 1925, 1931,
1936, 1942, 1953, 1959, 1964,
1970, 1981, 1987, 1992, 1998

GARDEN: CODE 0
1900, 1906, 1917, 1923, 1928,
1934, 1945, 1951, 1956, 1962,
1973, 1979, 1984, 1990

LIVING ROOM: CODE 4
1909, 1915, 1920, 1926, 1937,
1943, 1948, 1954, 1965, 1971,
1976, 1982, 1993, 1999

The setting for your party should consist of the six rooms and a garden. It doesn't have to be your own house, but each area must be distinct and have familiar associations: furniture, pictures, windows, and so on.

Use the Number-Shape System to remember the numbers of each room. So, imagine a golf club leaning against some book shelves in your study to help you remember the study is code 6.

The next stage is to convert each year into a person and work out where each person has been placed. If you have invested time in learning the Dominic System for the numbers 00 to 99, then you will have a list of 100 characters, and so you are already halfway there. As all the years are from the twentieth century, you need only convert the last two digits into a person, then imagine that person performing his or her action in their designated area of your home.

This will give you the code number (between 0 and 6) for the year you have been asked about. So, if someone says they were born in 1968, you imagine Stephen Hawking (68 = SH) looking through his telescope from the Bedroom, which gives you code 1.

THE CENTURY CODES

Perhaps you want to go one stage further by calculating dates from either the 19th century or 21st century. To calculate any day of the week from these centuries, simply carry out your calculation as normal – that is, add together the month date, the Month Code and the Year Code (you will need to read through to the end of page 117 to learn how to do this). When you arrive at your final total (see page 117) you will need to add to it another number – which I call a Century Code. Add 2 for the years 1800 to 1899. Add 6 for the years 2000 to 2099. Then continue the calculation as normal.

THE MONTH CODES

The second stage of the operation is to learn the numerical codes for the months. Here is a list of the numbers for each month:

SYSTEM: The Year Codes			
JANUARY	1	JULY	0
FEBRUARY	4	AUGUST	3
MARCH	4	SEPTEMBER	6
APRIL	0	OCTOBER	1
MAY	2	NOVEMBER	4
JUNE	5	DECEMBER	6

You must get to the point where you know the code for each month instantly. The best way to do this is to find an imaginative link between each month and its code number. Use mnemonics where necessary. For example, January is the first month. February makes me think of Four. For March I think of **march**ing 4-ward. April makes me think of April showers and I imagine **round** raindrops falling on me (number shape for zero).

May suggests to me a **two**-fold choice: that someone **may** or **may not** do something. June for me is a lady called **June** who's skirt has got caught on an **S-shaped hook** (number shape for 5). July sounds to me a bit like the word *jewel*, so I picture a jewel which is **round** in shape (number shape for zero).

August gives me a **gust** of wind, blowing **three** beach umbrellas over (since many people take beach vacations in August). September 6 happens to be my nephew's birthday. There is only **one** month in the year – October – that starts with the letter O. November makes me think of the **n**avy. I picture a sailor climbing up the **sail of a boat** (number shape for four). December makes me think of Christmas. I picture an elephant carrying a Christmas tree in his trunk (number shape for 6). Of course, my links may not work for you – in which case, you can create your own.

SYSTEM: The Year Codes			
SUNDAY	*1*	**THURSDAY**	**5**
MONDAY	**2**	**FRIDAY**	**6**
TUESDAY	**3**	**SATURDAY**	**0**
WEDNESDAY	**4**		

THE DAY CODES

Now all that's left to learn is the Day Code. All you need to know is that the week starts on a Sunday, hence 1, and ends with a Saturday, which you call zero. To reveal your Day Code, follow the calculation in the exercise opposite. For example, if your final figure is 15, cast out as many 7s as you can and see what you are left with. So, take 14 away from 15, leaving 1 – the Day Code for Sunday.

EXERCISE: Using the Codes to Reveal a Day of the Week

Now you can calculate any day of the week. Add together the date of the month (having cast out 7s), the Month Code and the Year Code. If the total is more than 7 – for example, 9 – again, cast out as many 7s as you can, leaving 2: a Monday. Now let's see how I calculated the day of that wedding on February 13th 1953:

1	*Date of the month: 13, cast out the 7*	= 6
2	*Month Code: February*	= 4
3	*Year Code: 1953 = EC = Eric Clapton*	
	(playing his guitar in your bathroom)	= 3
4	*Final total*	= 13
5	*By casting out 7s, this leaves us with 6*	
6	*What is the 6th day of the week?*	
	Answer: Friday – February 13th 1953 was a Friday	

Now, using the above codes see if you can calculate on which day of the week you, or someone close to you, was born.

CALCULATING LEAP YEARS AND OTHER CENTURIES

If a year leap is involved, then you'll need to make a slight alteration to your calculation, but only if the date falls between January 1st and February 29th. In this case, subtract 1 from your total before you cast out the 7s. If the leap-year date is outside January or February, carry out the calculation as usual.

Don't forget, for a day from the 19th or 21st centuries, you need to add the century code (see page 114) after step 3, above.

36   **How to Remember Historic Dates**

We can use the Dominic System combined with the three keys of memory – association, location and imagination – to memorize specific years in the twentieth century. All we need to do is convert numbers into persons and actions and link them to the events:

1   Let the description of the event suggest a key image.

2   Look at the date and convert the last two digits into the initials of a person, using the Dominic System (Steps 23, 31 and 33). You don't need to convert the first two digits as you know that all the dates are from the twentieth century.

3   Combine the key image with the person and their action to form a mental picture linking the two pieces of information.

The exercise opposite offers 15 notable years from the twentieth century. Let's use the three steps above to memorize the first date on the list together. First, the event suggests to me a simple image of a man stepping onto the moon's surface. Second, using the Dominic System, the last two digits of 1969 convert into the initials SN. So, I picture Sam Neill, running from a dinosaur, while taking his first step onto the moon's surface. Now the event and year are indelibly linked in a mental picture, which is firmly implanted in my memory.

EXERCISE: Twentieth-Century Historic Dates

Using the method we've just practised, allow yourself five minutes to commit to memory this list of 15 events and years:

EVENT	YEAR
First man on the moon	*1969*
Berlin Wall came down	*1989*
The Watergate break-in	*1972*
Bikini Atoll A-Bomb	*1946*
Mahatma Gandhi assassinated	*1948*
Start of Falklands War	*1982*
Sinking of Titanic	*1912*
Opening of the English Channel Tunnel	*1994*
Cuban Missile Crisis	*1962*
San Francisco Earthquake	*1906*
Yuri Gagarin is the first man in space	*1961*
Death of Elvis Presley	*1977*
Discovery of Penicillin	*1928*
The Hindenburg airship disaster	*1937*
Eruption of Mount St Helens	*1980*

Now cover the years and see how many of them you can remember correctly – write down the answers in your notebook.

Score *One point for each correct answer.*

Maximum points: 15   Untrained: 3+   Improver: 7+   Master: 14+

37 **Telephone Numbers and Important Dates**

If you have been using the Dominic System (Steps 23, 31 and 33), you should have a list of 100 characters, each with their own actions or props, representing all the two-digit numbers from 00 to 99. Once you are able to recognize any pair of digits as a person plus their action or prop, you will find the job of memorizing longer sequences of numbers much easier.

Each pair of numbers will always lead you to the initials of a particular person. With a little regular practice, recognizing two-digit numbers should become as easy as recognizing single Number Shapes. For example, whenever you see the number 43 you will automatically be reminded of the magician, David Copperfield (DC = 43), pulling a rabbit from a hat.

As a general rule, whatever number you need to memorize, place your character at a relevant location. For example, if you have a journey to make tomorrow, on the No. 43 bus, then use a bus stop as the site for your mnemonic image. You might picture David Copperfield, either waiting at the bus stop or driving the bus itself, no doubt pulling a rabbit out of a hat at the same time.

TELEPHONE NUMBERS

How then can we memorize a telephone number by using the Dominic System with a relevant location as a backdrop? Imagine you wish to memorize the number of your local hair salon:

HAIRDRESSING SALON TELEPHONE NUMBER – 226 8357

It's most likely you will already know the area code, so you will not need to include it in the number.

First, picture the inside of the salon you visit regularly. Next, work on the number itself by using the Dominic System to divide it into three pairs of digits, which become three familiar characters. For the last, single digit you can use the Number-Shape System:

22	=	*BRIGITTE BARDOT*
68	=	*STEPHEN HAWKING*
35	=	*CLINT EASTWOOD*
7	=	*BOOMERANG (NUMBER SHAPE FOR 7)*

Now you have something tangible to work with and all you need to do is link the characters together to make a short sequence.

For example, picture Brigitte Bardot pouting in her compact mirror as she enters the salon. She is greeted by Stephen Hawking, who is sitting at the reception desk – peering through his telescope. She then walks over to the salon chair, behind which Clint Eastwood is standing, and throwing a boomerang. The order in which you encounter the characters will ensure you remember the numbers in the correct sequence.

THE COMPLEX DOMINIC SYSTEM

Whether it's Mother's Day, a family birthday or your wedding anniversary, the same principle applies when remembering important dates as when remembering telephone numbers. The location you choose to anchor your mnemonic should be based around the person concerned. Let's say that your niece, Jessica, has an imminent birthday on November 8th. How can you remember it?

November 8th can be represented as 11.08. Using the Dominic System this gives us Andre Agassi (AA = 11) wearing a bowler hat (prop of Oliver Hardy = 08). You can base the scene at your niece's home. In this method the person (Andre Agassi) always represents the month, and the action or prop, the date.

But perhaps you express dates the other way round – date followed by month – for example, 8 November. In this case, your person will be Oliver Hardy (OH = 08), performing the action or prop of Andre Agassi (AA = 11), which is swinging a tennis racquet. Here, the person will always represent the date, and the action or prop, the month.

Notice how this time we have formed a complex image of one person and one action. One character has taken the action of the other. I call this the Complex Dominic System. Of course, we could have pictured both characters performing each of their actions. However, that scenario involves more work: two characters, plus two actions. Instead, we have combined the scene into one character and one action, thus creating a more succinct image, which is easier to fix in the mind.

EXERCISE: Using the Complex Dominic System

Below is a list of all the two-digit numbers arranged randomly, and grouped into pairs. Picture each pair as a person plus action or prop. Translate the numbers into letters, which will give you the initials of the person or person's action or prop. There is no need to write anything down. With practice, this process should become automatic.

76 16	61 68	97 33	42 88	36 27
96 08	20 59	10 77	30 04	65 83
06 52	35 00	55 81	99 26	03 53
89 72	57 32	07 51	49 73	39 43
62 60	12 56	31 05	75 82	66 85
21 09	29 80	34 95	41 90	67 84
17 87	71 25	58 47	44 28	63 11
94 79	01 74	38 18	23 70	91 40
86 15	92 46	22 19	24 48	69 93
98 37	64 14	45 02	50 78	13 54

38 **How to Remember the News**

Newspapers are valuable daily, and weekly, sources of information with which to practise your memory techniques. The challenge comes from the sheer miscellany of the material on offer – on one page, the details of a complex fraud case, on another proposals for a new record-breaking suspension bridge, and elsewhere an account of a territorial dispute between two foreign powers.

Newspapers, by their nature, trace the unfolding of events issue by issue – though not necessarily with great consistency. Stories can dominate the headlines for a week or so, then disappear, only to resurface with new developments at a later date, by which time we may have forgotten the finer points of the original story.

The exercise opposite gives you practice in following and recalling news stories – using in particular the Journey Method and Link Method. A typical news story involves dates, names (especially of foreign leaders), political parties, foreign alliances, statistics, and so on. This presents you with the challenge of selecting from your mnemonic repertoire the techniques that will be most appropriate for helping you to remember these different types of data. Absorbing these basic facts will enrich your understanding of the broader context of the story.

You might also consider using the financial pages of newspapers to test your ability to remember random digits. Or if you are a sports fan, you could perhaps try memorizing sporting league tables.

EXERCISE: The Great Paper Trail

This method will help you to retain the salient points of a number of news stories, as and when they are reported in your newspaper.

1 Try following, say, three separate and dissimilar stories for at least a month, or for as long as the stories run. Allocate a relevant journey to each story: for example, you might set an ecological story in your local park. Try to choose journeys to which you can add extra stages when needed. For example, perhaps the last stage of your journey to work can join up with the first stage of your journey to the gym.

2 As you read an article, sift the incidental from the essential. Focus on the issues, facts and events that you judge to be at the heart of the article.

3 Memorize the data using specific techniques: for example, Names and Faces (Step 16) for people, the Dominic System for statistics and numbers (Steps 23, 31 and 33), the Complex Dominic System for dates (Step 37; page 122), Countries and Capitals (Step 18) for place names, Remember Quotations (Step 27), and so on. Combine this data into a single complex scene – for example, a politician, at a certain time and place, giving a speech. Then place this image at a single stage of your journey.

4 Each time you read another article on your subject, first review your journey so far to check you can still remember the data you committed to memory last time. Once the news story has run its course, use the "rule of five" (Step 30) to revise and fix the information for the long term.

39 How to Memorize Oscar Winners

If you are one of those people who love the movies, then you may well be familiar with the Best Picture winners from the Oscars over the past few years. However, would you be able to name the year that one of them won the award? Take a look at the 30 Best Pictures from the Oscars for the years 1971 to 2000 listed below. How might you go about memorizing the dates and titles?

LIST: 30 Best Pictures from the Oscars 1971 to 2000

The French Connection	1971	Platoon	1986
The Godfather	1972	The Last Emperor	1987
The Sting	1973	Rain Man	1988
The Godfather Part II	1974	Driving Miss Daisy	1989
One Flew Over the Cuckoo's Nest	1975	Dances with Wolves	1990
Rocky	1976	The Silence of the Lambs	1991
Annie Hall	1977	Unforgiven	1992
The Deer Hunter	1978	Schindler's List	1993
Kramer vs. Kramer	1979	Forrest Gump	1994
Ordinary People	1980	Braveheart	1995
Chariots of Fire	1981	The English Patient	1996
Gandhi	1982	Titanic	1997
Terms of Endearment	1983	Shakespeare in Love	1998
Amadeus	1984	American Beauty	1999
Out of Africa	1985	Gladiator	2000

EXERCISE: 30 Best Picture Winners

To commit to memory the list of 30 Best Pictures from the Oscars on the opposite page, all that's required is a journey consisting of 30 stages. If this is information you might want to carry in your head for long-term storage, then I suggest you devise a route solely for this purpose – for example, one that starts at your local movie house.

Listed below are the first 10 stages of a journey that I would use to store the first 10 movies:

1	*Box Office*	*6*	*Screen Projector*
2	*Popcorn Counter*	*7*	*Restrooms*
3	*Cinema Screen*	*8*	*Bar Area*
4	*Front Row*	*9*	*Revolving Doors*
5	*Back Row*	*10*	*Taxicab Stand*

I would eventually extend my journey through my town. And I would make a mental note of the fifth, tenth, fifteenth, twentieth, twenty-fifth and thirtieth stages. That is, the back row, the taxicab stand, and so on. You'll see why shortly.

Then I would memorize the list of Best Pictures by translating each film into a key image and then planting each one at a different stage of the journey. So, at the first stage, I imagine someone with a distinctive French accent issuing my tickets. At the second stage, I picture my Godfather buying a large cup of popcorn. At the third stage, I imagine an enormous bee buzzing in front of the cinema screen, and so on.

test continued

You may have noticed that here, unlike when we were learning the years of historic events (see Step 36), we don't require the Dominic System to turn the years into characters. This is because I know that the movies follow a running order from 1971 to 2000 and the journey itself will fix this order in my mind.

I have made a mental note of certain stages along my route – the back row represents 1975, the taxi stand is 1980, and so on, until the year 2000, the thirtieth stage of my journey. This enables me to calculate any intervening year and its corresponding movie simply by jumping to these key stages along my journey, rather than having to run through the whole journey from the start.

Now create your own journey. Like me, you can begin in your local movie house and perhaps extend your route through the town, or you can choose a completely different journey. Don't forget to make a mental note of the fifth, tenth, fifteenth, twentieth, twenty-fifth and thirtieth stages.

Now copy the years into your notebook and try to write the corresponding Best Picture next to each year.

Score *One point for each correct answer.*
Maximum points: 30   Untrained: 5+   Improver: 24+   Master: 29+

You can also ask a friend to test you on random years, so that you can practise jumping to the key stages along your journey to recall the desired year.

40 **How to Remember Poetry**

The purpose of rhythm and rhyme is in part to make poetry memorable. We use the phrase "learning by heart", which is appropriate: if we really appreciate a piece of poetry – feeling it, understanding it and hearing its music – we are more likely to be word-perfect when we try to recite the verse either to ourselves or to others. But sadly, learning by heart is something few of us have the leisure for.

In this step I am going to show you how the Journey Method is an effective aid to memorizing poetry. When choosing the journey with which I will memorize a poem, open spaces often make the best locations. This is because I create several key images for each stage of my journey, and outdoor, uncluttered locations allow me to spread out my images.

The idea is to convert certain words from each line into key images that can be linked together and then mentally "placed" along each stage of the journey.

The exercise on the following pages lets you try this technique for yourself. At every stop along your journey ensure that you make an association between the location and the first word of the line of the poem, *plus* the actual subject of the line that you are trying to commit to memory. This is a tricky exercise, and depending on the complexity of the particular line, you may sometimes require several key images to remind you of the whole line, word for word. But don't panic, I'll start you off.

EXERCISE: Memorizing Lines of Poetry

I   Read through the following 14 lines of poetry – a sonnet – and choose a
    14-stage journey with a location relevant to the poem.

ODE TO THE WEST WIND BY PERCY BYSSHE SHELLEY

O WILD West Wind, thou breath of Autumn's being,	*(9)*
Thou from whose unseen presence the leaves dead	*(8)*
Are driven, like ghosts from an enchanter fleeing,	*(8)*
Yellow, and black, and pale, and hectic red,	*(8)*
Pestilence-stricken multitudes: O thou,	*(5)*
Who chariotest to their dark wintry bed	*(7)*
The wingèd seeds, where they lie cold and low,	*(9)*
Each like a corpse within its grave, until	*(8)*
Thine azure sister of the Spring shall blow	*(8)*
Her clarion o'er the dreaming earth, and fill	*(8)*
(Driving sweet buds like flocks to feed in air)	*(9)*
With living hues and odours plain and hill:	*(8)*
Wild Spirit, which art moving everywhere;	*(6)*
Destroyer and preserver; hear, oh hear!	*(6)*
Total number of words	*(107)*

2   Allow yourself 15 minutes to memorize as many words as you can from the first 14 lines of the poem.

3   At the start of your journey, picture a large ring or hoop in front of you. This will serve as a reliable cue for "O", the first word of the first line. To remind you of the line itself, choose a key image or scene which you think best represents it – a Wild West cowboy and a gust of Fall wind perhaps? Fuse the key images together and place them at the first stage of your journey. So, my starting position is the entrance to an autumnal woodland park, where I picture a large hoop, which I step through to see a Wild West cowboy being blown into the sky by a gust of wind.

4   At the second stage, form the next line prompter. What do you associate with the word "Thou"? Perhaps the word makes you think of a "Holier than Thou" preacher? Picture an image of a preacher crunching Fall leaves underfoot to remind you of the content of the second line of the poem.

5   At the third stage, you might choose to use the Alphabet System (Step 14) to remind you of the next line prompter "Are". Picture Romeo from *Romeo and Juliet* driving a car – he is chasing a cluster of ghosts, who are running away from a wizard ("enchanter"). And so on. Once you have memorized all 14 lines, see how many you can recall in your notebook.

Score *Add up the number of words you recalled correctly. Score one point for each word.*

Maximum points: 107   Untrained: 15+   Improver: 40+   Master: 100+

chapter 4

Memory Masterclass

Now you are into the final chapter of this book it's time to stretch the muscle of your memory to the limit. In some of the steps you will consolidate and expand on the techniques you have learned so far – for example, in Steps 41 (The Roman Room Method) and 43 (How to Store a Memory within a Memory) I will be teaching you extensions of the Journey Method to increase your journey's storage capacity. And in Step 46 I will be teaching you how to memorize multiple decks of cards, using the Complex Dominic System.

You will have the chance to try some of the challenges that are held at the World Memory Championships, such as the Binary Numbers test. These exercises are quite tough, but with the help of my new, advanced techniques – such as my unique Binary Code system (Step 44) for learning sequences of binary digits – I am confident that you will impress yourself.

In the last few steps of this chapter, I offer you games and tips for boosting your memory power, and there are revision exercises, too – so that you can brush up on your number memorization techniques. You will complete your training with some short tests in Step 52 to show you how much your memory power has improved since Step 1.

41 **The Roman Room Method**

In Step 10 you memorized a "to do" list of 10 jobs using a journey around your house or apartment. Do you still remember them? Telephone vet, mend sunglasses, bake cup cakes ... and so on.

If you can remember the list, then that's probably because you can still recall that original journey of 10 stages around your house. Using the same number of rooms, I am now going to show you how you can turn a 10-stage journey into one that can store five, 10, or even 50 times more items. This works by combining the Journey Method with the Roman Room Method.

The Roman Room Method works by using different objects or specific areas in a room as hooks or pegs to connect to the information you want to memorize: you could call it a journey within a journey. So, at the first stop along the journey around your home – the front door – you might choose the following five mini-stops: doorstep, mail box, doorbell, door handle and doorframe. It's a good idea to decide on a uniform direction around each room or area. In other words, the five objects should always be viewed in your mind's eye in, say, a clockwise direction.

If you are in a room right now, look around you from left to right. How many objects can you count? Perhaps there is a table, chair, window, television, and two or more pictures on the wall. If you think about it, there are probably hundreds if not thousands of pieces of furniture, appliances, trinkets, cooking utensils, books, and so on, that you could use to link to a list of hundreds of items.

EXERCISE: The Roman Room

In the following exercise you will see a list of 50 shopping items (on the following page) which I am going to ask you to memorize by looking at each item only once. There is no need to extend the existing journey around your home from the original 10 stages. Instead, choose five objects, pieces of furniture or small areas from each room, to increase your memory storage space to 50.

Once you have prepared a journey of 10 stops, each with five mini-stops, and you are confident that you know all 50 places in sequence, then allow yourself no more than 15 minutes to memorize the list of 50 shopping items on the following page.

Work through from beginning to end making links between the items and the objects in your home, and avoid the temptation to go back over your links to cement them further. Have faith in your imagination and trust that the combination of the journey and the use of imaginative association will firmly lodge this list directly into your long-term memory. Only when you get to the end should you review the list to strengthen the links you made.

 *test continued*

SHOPPING LIST

1	Potted plant	18	Perfume	35	Wine glasses
2	Loaf of bread	19	Ballet shoes	36	Beer
3	Adhesive tape	20	Soft toy	37	Peaches
4	Butter	21	Key ring	38	Eggs
5	Sausages	22	Pencils	39	Salmon
6	Cookbook	23	CD	40	Nails
7	Coffee beans	24	Dog collar	41	Wicker basket
8	Peppergrinder	25	Hammer	42	Yogurt
9	Light bulb	26	Newspaper	43	Candles
10	Suitcase	27	Milk	44	Lamp stand
11	Toothbrush	28	Tulips	45	Golf club
12	Scissors	29	Laptop	46	Map
13	Batteries	30	Camera	47	Playing cards
14	Soap	31	Gold bracelet	48	Blue balloons
15	Needles	32	Ice cream	49	Calculator
16	Bicycle pump	33	Pillowcase	50	Red paint
17	Vase	34	Kite		

Let's try the first stage together. How would you link the first five items on your shopping list with the first five mini-stops on your journey? You could begin by picturing yourself standing on your doorstep, where there is a large potted plant that you have to step over. Next you see a loaf of bread sticking out of your mailbox. You notice that your doorbell is taped up with adhesive tape. Your hand slips when you try turning the door handle, as it is dripping with butter. Once you manage to open your door, you see a string of sausages dangling from the top of the doorframe.

Now move onto the second stage of your journey and place the next five items at your next five mini-stops, and so on, right to the end of the list.

Now see how many items you can recall. Write down as many as you can, in sequence, in your notebook. This is a very difficult test and I am not expecting you to recall anywhere near the 50 correct items.

Score *Two point for each shopping item remembered.*

Maximum points: 100   Untrained: 5+   Improver: 22+   Master: 90+

42 **How to Remember Historic and Future Dates**

In Step 36 we learned how to memorize dates from the twentieth century. We used the Dominic System to convert the last two digits of the year into a person. However, if we wish to memorize historic and future dates (that is, dates from other centuries), then we need to remember all four digits of the particular year.

To do this I use the Complex Dominic System (see page 122) to convert the year into a complex image (person, plus action). Then, as in Step 36, I find a way of connecting this image to the event. I pick key images (or sometimes words) from each event to link to the year. Let's use a fictitious event as an example: imagine that in 1808 a chimpanzee became the first animal to memorize a deck of playing cards. How would I memorize this? First, I translate the year date, 1808, into Adolph Hitler (AH = 18) wearing a bowler hat (prop of Oliver Hardy; OH = 08). Then I pick the key image of a chimpanzee holding a deck of cards to represent the event. Next I need an appropriate location to store these images and link them together in a scene. I store the image of Adolph Hitler wearing a bowler hat in the monkey house, where the chimpanzee is holding a deck of cards. By carrying out this imaginative process, the event and its date are now so vividly imprinted in your memory you are unlikely to forget them. However, as a further aid for retrieving this type of memory in the first place, you may wish to create a journey along which you place each event.

EXERCISE: Historic and Future Dates

Allow yourself five minutes to memorize the following list of 15 dates and fictitious events. Use a 15-stage journey if you wish.

	EVENT	YEAR
1	*First time machine invented*	1911
2	*Flying camels become extinct*	1234
3	*Women rule the world*	2078
4	*Musician eats his own piano*	1444
5	*Atlantis discovered at South Pole*	1612
6	*Man-eating frogs invade Malta*	1893
7	*Octopus ink holds key to eternal youth*	1759
8	*Potatoes more valuable than gold*	2023
9	*Paris designated a juggling-free zone*	1065
10	*The greeting "hello" is used for the first time*	1130
11	*Talking bicycles are the height of fashion*	1342
12	*Guitar used as bow and arrow*	1276
13	*Elm tree elected as president of Peru*	2064
14	*Underwater fire found to be non-hazardous*	1489
15	*Man armed with pen killed by sword*	1998

Now cover this page and see how many of the events and their respective years you can list in your notebook.

Score *One point for each correct answer.*

Maximum points: 15   Untrained: 3+   Improver: 9+   Master: 14+

43 How to Store a Memory within a Memory

In Step 41 we saw how the Roman Room Method acts as a journey within a journey. It uses different objects in a room as hooks or pegs to connect to the information you want to memorize. Now we shall be using the actual items from any list you wish to memorize as the hooks to connect to *other* items you wish to remember: in other words, you will be storing a memory within a memory.

Let's work through a very short example together, using the two unrelated columns of words in the box below.

Work down the list of names and picture someone you know – or somebody famous – with the same name at each stage along your journey. Don't forget to use your imagination: if you can't think of anyone called Rosie, you could picture a rosebush instead. Once you have stored the names, review the journey,

ROSIE	*PEBBLE*
CHRIS	*LAUGHTER*

only this time use each person as a peg to attach a word (from the second column) to. So, if you placed Rosie (or a rosebush) at the first stage of your journey (say, your front door), now you picture her, still standing at your front door, only this time, holding a pebble (or a pebble under the rosebush). At the second stage of your journey, you again find Chris waiting for you, but now you picture Chris laughing.

EXERCISE: Memories within Memories

Now try memorizing the lists of 20 names and 20 nouns, below, one column at a time. You are combining the Journey Method with your powerful imagination to create memorable associations.

NAME	NOUS
CAROLINE	MAGAZINE
REBECCA	TELEPHONE
CHARLIE	KISS
ANNE	FLIGHT
SARAH	FICTION
DAVID	ANGER
RUPERT	PAINTER
JESSE	HOSTESS
PETER	SLEEP
MARY	WISHBONE
BILL	DIZZINESS
JANE	SONG
SAM	HOUR
EDWARD	CHEF
ANNE	PIANO
STEVE	STAIRWAY
ANDY	PUNCH
KIRSTEN	HAND
DOMINIC	CARDS
SALLY	DANCER

test continued

I   Prepare a 20-stage journey. Work down the list of names, visualizing one person, or an image representing their name, at each stage of the journey.

2   Once you have stored all 20 names, run through the journey again, this time linking the nouns to the people.

3   When you have stored all 20 combined images of people and nouns, allow yourself two minutes to review the whole journey. Then cover page 141, and allow yourself five minutes to reproduce the two columns of items in your notebook.

Score *One point for each correct person and one point for each correct noun.*
Maximum points: 40   Untrained: 8+   Improver: 26+   Master: 38+

If you scored 13 or more, you may wish to test yourself further. Have a friend ask you a quick-fire round of 20 random questions about any of the 40 words in the two lists. For example, "Who do you associate with anger?", "Who is the eighteenth person on the list and what is their associated noun?" or "What person comes immediately before the person whose associated noun is Song?" This will demonstrate how fluent you now are at scanning back and forth through a journey, and retrieving multiple pieces of information from it.

This exercise demonstrates how, in theory, you could keep adding new columns of data ad infinitum. For example, Caroline reading a magazine about Chinese violinists, and so on.

44 How to Memorize Binary Numbers

Binary is the language of computers. In mathematics it is a base-2 numbering system using combinations of the digits 0 and 1 to represent all values. It is one of the simplest ways of representing information because only two symbols, 0 and 1, are employed.

The Binary test is one of the key events at the World Memory Championships. In 2004 the Englishman Ben Pridmore set a new world record by memorizing 3,705 binary digits in 30 minutes.

If you have learned the Dominic System for all the numbers from 00 to 99 then you already have the tool for memorizing binary numbers. The following system allows you to remember a 12-digit binary number using the Complex Dominic System to form a single image (using one person and one action/prop).

THE BINARY CODE

When presented with a string of zeroes and ones, we must first break it down into a series of smaller groups of three digits each. For reasons that will become apparent, you must then ascribe a single-digit, base-10 number to each group. Below I have listed the eight different three-digit binary numbers, together with their new single-digit, base-10 number:

000 = 0	*011 = 2*	*110 = 4*	*010 = 6*
001 = 1	*111 = 3*	*100 = 5*	*101 = 7*

Learn this simple code: the codes for the numbers 0 to 3 are easily remembered – two 1's make 2, three 1's make 3, and so on. But the codes for the numbers 4 to 7 are more difficult. You could use visual mnemonics to remember these codes. For example, 110 makes me think of a golf ball rolling toward two people – I shout "Fore!" to warn them. 100 looks a little like a pair of glasses – I put them on to inspect a seahorse (a number shape for 5). 010 might remind you of an elephant – two ears either side of a trunk (a number shape for 6). 101 resembles a dinner plate with a knife and fork either side: I tend to eat at 7pm most evenings.

You can now represent any three-digit binary number with a single-digit, base-10 number. It follows that six-digit binary numbers can be represented by a two-digit, base-10 number. For example:

> ***101 = 7 and 011 = 2   Therefore   101011 = 72***
>
> ***110 = 4 and 111 = 3   Therefore   110111 = 43***

If you now convert these numbers into a person and action using the Dominic System what complex image do you get? Mine is of George Bush (72 = GB) pulling a rabbit out of a hat (43 = action of DC: David Copperfield.) Now you have memorized a 12-digit binary number – 101011110111 – with a single complex image.

EXERCISE: The Binary Challenge

Here is a random sequence of 60 binary digits. To memorize this sequence you could use a journey of 10 stages to convert 10 sets of six digits into a person. Better still, by converting them into a complex image of a person and action you would need only a five-stage journey. For example, the first set of six digits 011 110 can be represented by the two-digit, base-10 number 24 (011 = 2 and 110 = 4). The second set of six digits becomes the two-digit base-10 number 36 (111 = 3 and 010 = 6). You might picture Bob Dylan (24 = BD) striding along a catwalk (36 = action of CS: Claudia Schiffer).

Allow yourself 15 minutes to commit the sequence to memory.

011 110 111 010 111 100 000 001 101 111 100 001 010 101 101 100 111 000 110 010

Now try to write down as much of the sequence as you can in your notebook.

Score *One point for each correct binary number. As in the Binary Numbers test at the start of this book (see page 14), this is a "sudden death" challenge – if you recall the first six digits correctly, then make a mistake on the seventh digit, your score is six.*

Maximum points: 60   *Untrained: 6+*   *Improver: 12+*   *Master: 42+*

Don't worry if you didn't score very highly – this is a phenomenally difficult exercise. Keep practising this method by setting yourself new sequences of binary numbers.

45 **How to Memorize a Dictionary**

A few years ago I visited Malaysia and gave a presentation on memory to an invited audience. I was joined by the Malaysian National Memory champion, Dr Yip Swe Chooi, who gave a demonstration of dictionary memorization.

Dr Yip, like me, had discovered the power of using the Journey Method to store information, only he decided to take his memory journeys to extraordinary lengths, literally.

He told me that he had spent several months memorizing an English-Chinese dictionary of approximately 58,000 entries. Not only did he claim to know the entire sequence, but also that given any English word he could provide both the definition of the word and its Chinese translation. I decided to put him to the test and gave him the word "upholstery". To my surprise, within a few seconds he was able to give me a precise definition of the word and the correct Chinese translation, plus the page number and where the entry fell on that page. Other members of the audience also put Yip to the test, and each time he answered correctly. Dr Yip tells me that he has one long journey consisting of 58,000 stages and at every stage he is able to access the data in the form of key imagery.

Dr Yip's demonstration ranks as one of the most impressive memory feats I have ever witnessed. Apart from the great practical benefit of being a walking dictionary, Yip's feat is a testament to the limitless nature of human memory and gives us definitive proof of the Journey Method's awesome power.

EXERCISE: The Random Word Challenge

Although you will be relieved to learn that I am not going to ask you to memorize the English-Swahili Dictionary, the following exercise will test your powers of association to the limit.

The Random Word event held at the World Memory Championships involves competitors memorizing as many random words as possible in sequence in 15 minutes. The 80 words listed on the following page are the first 80 words from the Random Word event at the actual championships a few years ago.

You decide how best to organize your journey for this. Personally I use one stage of my journey to link to one word, so I require an 80-stage journey. However, I do know competitors who link two words together and then position them at one stage of the route, which means that they need a 40-stage journey (see Step 43; How to Store a Memory within a Memory). Alternatively, you could use the Roman Room Method (see Step 41). Simply extend the journey around your home to include 16 stages, each with five mini-stages.

After you have prepared your journey, turn the page and allow yourself 15 minutes to memorize as many words as you can, in sequence.

Hint: Spend about 10 minutes memorizing as many words as you can, then in the last five minutes review what you have stored.

 test continued

80 WORDS FROM THE RANDOM WORD EVENT

dissect	bleed	arrange	scissors	kilt
pig	pilot	slam	banana	over
phase	consort	smitten	broom	hairbrush
coconut	cosy	paving	cubicle	parlour
baboon	base	indicate	gammon	sleigh
oral	crisp	follow	denture	oven
armour	pier	trolley	log	sibling
sawdust	grid	arcade	glove	cannon
italic	escort	giraffe	atomic	watch
energy	heresy	commission	redundant	pretender
orange	bone	duck	swallow	certificates
bureau	argument	slalom	befriend	confess
ivory	gamma	permissive	skull	moth
pocket	parrot	implode	bunker	dynamite
accountant	boss	franchise	six	reform
tension	reckon	fish	pay	suppress

Now try to recall as many words as you can, in sequence, by writing them down in your notebook.

Score One point for each consecutive word you can remember from the first word on the list onward, before a mistake is made.

Maximum points: 80   Untrained: 5+   Improver: 20+   Master: 50+

46 **How to Memorize Multiple Decks of Cards**

On July 21st 1985, Creighton Carvello, the great man who inspired me to train my memory, appeared on the Japanese edition of the television show, "Guinness World of Records".

This was a live show and when Creighton came on stage to perform a feat of card memorization, something extraordinary happened. In Creighton's own words:

"My intention was to memorize six separate decks of cards, but when my memorization started I noticed the cards hadn't been shuffled enough and were mostly still in sequence. So the girls from Japanese TV started shuffling them again, but the cards fell off the table onto the floor. They were picked up all jumbled up in a pile, then reshuffled, with all six decks in one random pile. I only had a single sighting of all 312 cards and made 24 errors on the recall. So a new record was born: six decks of cards all shuffled together instead of 6 separate decks!"

Since that time, I and other card memorizers around the world have for years been battling it out, memorizing more and more decks to see how far we can take Creighton's original record.

In 2002 I memorized the order of 54 decks (2,808 cards) that had been shuffled into each other and dealt out just once. I made eight errors on the recall and this, at the time of writing this book, still stands as the current World Record for multiple-deck memorization. This is how I memorized the 54 decks:

I used the Journey Method combined with the Complex Dominic System. First, I prepared 27 journeys each with 52 stages or stops along the way. Then at each stage of the journey I imagined seeing a person and action which represented two cards. In other words, I had 1,404 stages each storing a complex image comprising two playing cards.

For example, if the first two cards to be dealt out were the King of Diamonds followed by the Ace of Clubs I would picture Bill Gates (my King of Diamonds) carrying a bottle of liquor (the action of Al Capone, who is my Ace of Clubs), and he would be standing at my front door, the first stage of my first journey. If the cards were in reverse, then I would have pictured Al Capone counting his diamonds (the action of Bill Gates), standing at my front door.

If you attempted to memorize a deck of playing cards in Step 34, then you will already have a journey of 52 stages, so in theory you will have enough mental storage space to memorize two decks. Of course, another way of looking at it is that you only need a 26-stage journey to memorize one deck, as opposed to the 52 stages you used in Step 34.

Before you try memorizing two decks, you may wish to review your Dominic System (Steps 23, 31 and 33) and your face cards (Step 34; page 110) to ensure that your playing card characters are fixed freshly in your mind.

EXERCISE: Two Decks of Playing Cards

Now try to memorize two decks of cards, using the Journey Method and the Complex Dominic System, as I have just explained.

1   Run through your journey from Step 34 and make sure you are familiar with all of the 52 stages.

2   Shuffle the two decks of cards together. As you deal out the cards, convert each pair of cards into a single complex image (person and action) and place it at a stage along your journey.

3   Allow yourself 15 minutes to try to memorize the two decks.

4   Now try to recall all 104 cards. Either ask a friend to listen as you call out each card in sequence or repeat the sequence by writing it down in your notebook.

Score Measure your success by the number of errors you make, if any.

Maximum errors: 104   Untrained: 42+   Improver: 41 or less   Master: 9 or less

Don't worry if you found this exercise difficult. If you made 42 or more errors, practise regularly with a single deck of cards (see page 111) and move onto two decks again when you feel ready. If you made, say, 20 or fewer errors, you may wish to have a go at memorizing multiple decks of cards. For example, to memorize four decks of cards, you will need to prepare a new 52-stage journey to store the next set of complex images.

47 How to Memorize a Room Full of People

When I am giving a presentation or after-dinner speech I usually finish off with my "party trick" of naming everyone in the room. Perhaps you attend business conventions or big charity dinners where you meet a lot of new people at once. In Step 15 we learned how to remember people's names and faces by noticing physical resemblances, distinctive facial features, "sound-alike" names, and so on – and, in all of these cases, placing the image you have created in a relevant location. You may wish to review Step 15 before continuing with this step.

Here I am going to show you what to do when you are given a person's name – or lots of people's names – before you have met them: for example, when you are sent a list of attendees with your conference pack, or when you look at the seating plan at a wedding. First, choose a suitable journey with the correct number of stages, let's say 50. If the list of 50 names is grouped in some way, perhaps a seating plan of five people per table, or five conference delegates from one company or country, you may wish to use 10 separate five-stage journeys, or you could use a journey of 10 stages each with five mini-stages (see the Roman Room Method; Step 41). So, Table One would be the first room on your journey, Table Two the second, and so on. If they are grouped according to a company name, visualize the company – for example, for "Tiger Shipping" I might visualize a ship painted with black and orange tiger stripes pinned to the door of the room.

Let's imagine that the first name on the list is Victoria Green. Even though we haven't met Victoria Green yet – and thus have no physical resemblances or characteristics to draw upon – we need to create an image to represent her name. Victoria makes me think of Queen Victoria of England. I picture Queen Victoria wearing a bright green dress, and I place this image at the first stage of my journey. When I meet the real Victoria Green, I integrate her into my image – I picture her curtseying to Queen Victoria. Now you'll have no problem remembering Victoria for the rest of the evening.

However, let's say you notice a distinctive feature or resemblance when you finally meet Victoria in person. You can use this to reinforce still further the link between the real person and your imaginary scene. Perhaps she has a dazzling smile: if so, make sure Victoria is smiling at Queen Victoria in your image.

I would work through the entire list of 50 people in the same way, placing each as-yet-unknown person at a stage or mini-stage of my journey. Then when I meet the person I find some creative way to integrate them into my existing scene.

Let's say you want to use all your memorized names as a party trick, as I often do. Ask everyone to stand up. Walk around the room and name everyone individually – each person sits down as they hear their name. Anyone left standing must be a gatecrasher!

EXERCISE: Guests' Names and Seating Plans

Imagine you are attending a formal dinner and you are looking at four table plans and the names of 20 guests. Try to memorize all 20 names and their table numbers. First, select either four separate journeys of five stages each or one journey of four stages with five mini-stages at each stop (the Roman Room Method). Then, use your powers of imagination to turn each person's name into key images or scenes and place them at a stage or mini-stage along your journey(s).

TABLE 1	TABLE 2	TABLE 3	TABLE 4
Jane Little	Mike Stetson	Steve Ranger	Eve Rowe
Peter Lyons	Jill Taylor	June Harvey	Rupert Watts
Sally Bishop	Bill Hatcher	Andy Cushion	Nina Harley
Henry Whale	Fred Noble	Lilly Bedding	Terry Ward
Susan Dance	Mary Brown	Dave Lark	Rowena Ward

Now see if you can remember which guest is sitting at which table. Write down the table number, followed by the five guests, in your notebook.

Score Five points for each correctly remembered guest (you must recall both the first name and surname to score).

Maximum points: 100   Untrained: 15+   Improver: 50+   Master: 90+

48 **Healthy Body, Healthy Memory**

So far throughout this book you have been training your memory by working on your mind: stretching it to the limit with a variety of challenging exercises. Mental exercise is imperative if you wish to achieve improvements in memory power, but the other part of you should not be ignored. In other words, by exercising your body, too, you will maximize the effects of your memory training.

Over the years I have observed that the competitors who perform particularly well in memory competitions are those who appear relaxed and physically fit. Of course, there are exceptions, but I can say from experience that my best performances have tended to follow a period of physical as well as mental training.

Our brains thrive on oxygen, and I believe the most productive way to help transport oxygen to the brain cells is through regular physical exercise. I'm not suggesting this necessitates running a half-marathon every week, but any form of exercise that can gently raise your heart rate and leave you feeling slightly out

of breath is better than nothing. Aim to perform some form of physical exercise for about twenty minutes a day.

Diet also plays a part in helping to keep our memory in full working order. Foods that are rich in the antioxidant vitamins A, C and E have been shown to aid memory. These vitamins are found in richly coloured fruit and vegetables, such as bananas, red peppers, spinach and oranges. They help to mop up chemicals known as free radicals, which can cause cell damage in the brain. Oily fish, such as salmon, contains folic acid and several essential fatty acids (in particular omega-3 oils), all of which are vital for maintaining a healthy brain and nervous system. Nutritional supplements such as

Ginkgo Biloba, which I take, can help transport oxygen to the brain cells.

STRESS AND STIMULATION

Many of the people who have sought training from me do so in the belief that memory techniques alone will solve all their problems relating to memory. However, upon investigation, what appears to lie at the heart of a decline in their memory is a substantial increase in stress in their lives. Whilst I encourage these people to train regularly with the techniques outlined in this book, I also help them to identify what may be the causes of their stress.

In stressful situations the body produces large amounts of adrenaline. This is a primitive survival mechanism known as the "flight or fright" response. However, in most stressful situations today, this reaction is redundant, and so the adrenaline is not burned off – it continues to build up in our bodies. Exposure to prolonged or excessive stress is highly damaging to memory.

Not only does the brain stop producing new neurons as a result of stress, but the corresponding lack of mental stimulation can cause existing neurons to die. We need to strike a balance between stimulating and nurturing our minds, and protecting them against the perils of stress.

TIPS: Stress-busting

The following tips are designed to help you release tension and combat stress.

- Exercise your mind and body regularly. Play mind games to stimulate your brain and physical games to treat your brain to a regular dose of oxygen.

- Eat a balanced diet high in antioxidants (vitamins A, C and E) and essential fatty acids found in oily fish, nuts and seeds.

- Make time for regular relaxation each day. This can be anything that makes you feel calm, such as a warm bath, a country walk or painting a picture.

- When you are feeling under pressure, practise a memory meditation. Close your eyes and pick a positive memory, perhaps a special day out or a beautiful landscape. Visualize a single image which captures this memory. Imagine that all the positive emotions you felt at the time are emanating from it. When you open your eyes you will feel re-energized and focused.

- Keep a stress journal to help you identify the causes and patterns of stress. In your notebook, allocate a page for each day of the week. Jot down when you feel stressed, and what occurred just before you experienced stress. Also, note down all your activities and how you were feeling at the time. At the end of the week, assess your journal. Are any patterns emerging? If you felt most stressed on your commute to work, you might consider alternative modes of transport. If you felt most relaxed when spending time with your family, try to schedule more family time.

49   **How to Win at Quiz Games**

People who have faith in the notion of general knowledge usually love quizzes – whether in magazines, bars or clubs, or with popular board games such as Trivial Pursuit. Even if you're not a quiz fan, memorizing the kinds of information quiz masters ask about is a great way to practise your memory techniques.

The basic method you will be using involves three stages. One or more key words in the question will lead you to a location. The answer to the question will then conjure an image. And your vivid imagination will link the two. Let's look at an example:

> **Q:**   *What is the alternative name for a cavy?*
>
> **A:**   Guinea pig

The key word here is "cavy", which sounds a bit like cave. I use a cave I know in the south of France as the location. I picture

a large guinea pig coming out of the mouth of the cave.

This method appears deceptively simple. The difficulty arises from the sheer variety of information you are dealing with. Another challenge will be selecting the essential key words in the question. Often, there will be more key words than you need. Use the Dominic System (Steps 23, 31 and 33) to remember numbers and dates. Use Steps 15 and 47 for names and people.

EXERCISE: Trivia Questions and Answers

Try learning the answers to the following questions. For the first question I would pick the key words "baking" and "Henry Jones". I picture my local bakery store, with bags of flour floating in the air, and a man behind the counter (Henry Jones), whose name I commit to memory, using the techniques in Step 47. The year 1845 can then be disregarded. However, had I chosen to work with "1845" instead of "Henry Jones", I would use the Complex Dominic System to convert the man behind the counter into Adolf Hitler conducting music.

QUESTION	ANSWER
1 *What aid to baking was invented in 1845 by Henry Jones?*	Self-raising flour
2 *Which planet was orbited by Mariner Nine in 1972?*	Mars
3 *What kind of clock was invented by scientist Christian Huygens?*	Pendulum clock
4 *Which is the only year last century to have seen three different Popes?*	1978
5 *Who played Batman in the 1989 film version?*	Michael Keaton
6 *Which continent has the lowest highest mountain?*	Australia
7 *What type of bird is a Canvasback?*	A duck

Score Now cover the answers and see how many questions you can answer correctly – jot the answers down in your notebook. How did you do? At this stage I would expect you to be able to answer every question correctly.

50 Games to Boost Your Memory Power

It's never too early or too late to start training one's memory. I can remember as a young child playing a memory game with my mother whenever we travelled a great distance in the car. Although we played it to relieve the boredom of the journey, I believe this may have planted the seeds of my future career. Whatever its official name, my mother referred to the game as "When I went down to the seaside".

She would start the game and say something like, "When I went down to the seaside, I packed in my bag a snorkel." Then I would repeat the sentence, adding another item to the list: "When I went down to the seaside, I packed a snorkel and a pair of sunglasses." The game would progress like this – my mother and I taking turns to repeat the previous list, each time adding a further item – until one of us forgot a link or made a mistake in the sequence of items.

Combining memory with a game in this way is a great way of sharpening concentration as well as improving your recall.

Another memory game that kept me entertained for hours was a card game called Pelminism or "Pairs". This involves dealing out a deck of 52 playing cards face down in four rows of 13 cards. The aim of the game is to win more matching pairs of cards (two aces, two sevens, and so on) than one's opponent. Players take turns to turn over two cards and, if they reveal a match, then they win that pair of cards, removing the pair from the game and taking a free turn. If a player turns over two different cards, then they replace them face down in the same position and it is the next player's turn. The person who can recall the position of the most cards from previous turns will reveal the most pairs and win the game.

A popular memory game played at parties and one used in many Boy Scout camps is "Kim's game", taken from the Rudyard Kipling novel *Kim*. There are several variations of this game but essentially a nominated games master collects 20 objects, usually kitchen items, and places them on a tray covered with a towel or cloth. The cover is then removed and players are allowed one minute to memorize as many of the items as possible.

TEST: Kim's Game

Here is a more challenging version of "Kim's game" for you to play with a friend. Ask your friend to arrange 20 household items on a table, covered. Uncover the items and allow yourself one minute to memorize all 20 objects. Then turn your back and ask your friend to remove four or five items. Now turn round and try to name the missing items. If, like me, you use a tried and tested 20-stage journey to place the items along, then you should have a distinctly unfair advantage over someone with an untrained memory.

Score At this stage of the book I would expect you to be able to name all the missing items. If you did, then you have made remarkable progress with your memory.

51 **Number Memorization Exercises**

The following exercises are revision exercises for the various number techniques you have learned in this book, aimed to speed up the process of translating numbers into mnemonic images. Let's start by refreshing your memory of single digits:

EXERCISE: Practising Single-digit Number Conversions

On the opposite page are 70 single-digit numbers between 0 and 9. The aim is not to memorize the rows of numbers, but to revise number shapes or rhymes until they become instantaneous. You can read the rows of numbers vertically or horizontally as you wish.

Read through the list of single-digit numbers, converting each one into its corresponding Number Shape (Step 12) or Number Rhyme (Step 13), depending on your preference. (As this is a visual exercise I personally find the Number-Shape System works best here.)

There is no need to write anything down. Just try to picture the image and, if it helps, name the image to yourself. For example, whenever you see the number 7, say "boomerang" to yourself and try to picture a boomerang.

Start slowly, reading through the numbers and forming images as you go. Then gradually speed up, as the conversion process becomes more automatic. Your aim is to reach the stage where images are triggered by a flash of each digit:

2	4	3	9	7	1	0
5	7	1	1	4	2	8
7	3	5	4	6	0	9
1	0	2	8	0	4	7
8	1	6	2	2	5	5
3	2	8	7	9	6	6
9	6	7	5	8	7	7
1	9	4	3	5	8	4
0	5	0	6	3	9	2
7	4	9	0	1	3	3

Pause

Now repeat this exercise, but try speeding up a little. This time you should be able to successfully convert every number into a Number Shape or Number Rhythm within five minutes.

TWO-DIGIT CONVERSIONS

If you have learned the complete Dominic System (Steps 23, 31 and 33), then you should be able to recognize any two-digit number from 00 to 99 as a person with their accompanying unique action or prop. The following exercise is designed to help you practise converting numbers into your Dominic System characters.

EXERCISE: Practising Two-digit Number Conversions

Below is a list of all the two-digit numbers from 00 to 99, arranged randomly. First, read through the list and simply picture each two-digit number as a person – don't worry about actions or props, as we'll work on these in a minute. Again, there is no need to write anything down. You are not attempting to memorize the list of numbers: all you are trying to do is to put a face to each two-digit number.

08	14	51	07	17	74	78	69	10	36
16	68	66	33	99	12	39	53	09	85
91	93	47	76	28	25	42	80	63	98
24	87	82	92	21	62	06	59	29	97
35	77	94	88	05	13	45	44	95	61
72	26	34	90	40	60	55	15	30	79
50	56	43	19	49	27	70	84	46	54
11	20	67	03	58	83	38	04	31	18
37	65	00	89	71	22	86	01	23	64
32	96	57	41	73	75	02	81	48	52

Now that those people are fresh in your mind, work your way through the list again and this time try to visualize, in as much detail as you can, the same people with their props or performing their characteristic actions.

Practise for a few minutes each day until you reach the point where you can "see" two-digit numbers automatically as people

EXERCISE: Practising the Complex Dominic System

In Step 4, I taught you a mnemonic for recalling Pi to the first few decimal places. Here I want you to memorize Pi to the first 20 decimal places (below), using a journey and the Complex Dominic System.

3.I **4 I 5 9 2 6 5 3 5 8 9 7 9 3 2 3 8 4 6**

Choose a five-stage journey. Then, using the Complex Dominic System, take five minutes to memorize a person, plus an action or prop, for each group of four digits along your route. Now reproduce the numbers in your notebook.

Score *You are now almost at the end of this 52-step program and I would expect you to remember all the first 20 decimal places to Pi correctly.*

If you wish to practise further at converting numbers into complex images, then keep working at the exercise in Step 37 (page 123).

52 How Brilliant is Your Memory Now?

In Step 1 you took several tests to assess your untrained memory power. Now that you've reached Step 52, take the following tests to see how much your memory power has improved.

TEST 1: Words

Study this list of 20 words for three minutes. Recall as many of the words as you can. The order is not important. Score one point for each correct word.

GIRL   ROPE   CAKE   LEAF

HORSE   BEARD   SUGAR   SCARF

LEATHER   HAMMER   DRAGON   FEATHER

BANANA   ARROW   CLOCK   SALMON

BRICK   BOOK   STOOL   RADIO

TEST 2: Number Sequence

Allow yourself three minutes to memorize the following sequence of 20 digits. Then reproduce as many numbers as you can, in sequence. Score one point for each correct digit. As in Step 1, this is "sudden death". In other words, if you recall all 20 digits but the seventh digit is incorrect, your score is six.

3 8 7 0 3 3 5 5 6 2 3 4 9 1 9 9 4 2 8 1

TEST 3: Names and Faces

Take three minutes to study the following 10 names and faces.

| DAVID LACE | MARY PETERS | DOMINIC FIELDS | THERESA FORD | STEVE LITTLEJOHN |
| ANNE LARCH | PAUL BASS | JAMES PICKLES | RICHARD SINGER | JILL HOOK |

Now cover the names and faces above and look at the same 10 faces in a different sequence below. Try to fill in the correct name for each person. Score five points for each correct first name and five points for each correct surname.

TEST 4: Playing Cards

Take three minutes to study the following 10 playing cards, then try to recall the exact sequence. As with the number sequence in Test 2, this is "sudden death". Score one point for each card you can recall before making a mistake.

TEST 5: Shapes

Take three minutes to memorize the following sequence of 10 shapes.

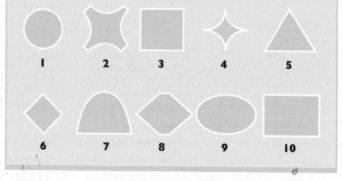

Here the shapes are in a new order. Cover page 168, then try to number them in their original order. Score one point for each correctly numbered shape.

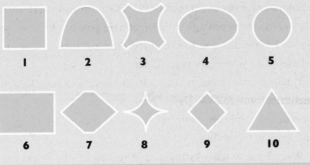

TEST 6: Binary numbers

Take three minutes to memorize the sequence of 30 binary numbers below, then try to reproduce as many of the sequence as you can before a mistake is made. Score one point for each correct number. Again, this is "sudden death".

1 0 1 0 1 1 0 0 0 1 0 1 1 1 1 0 1 0 0 1 1 1 0 1 1 0 0 1 0 1

Score *Now add up the scores from the six tests to arrive at a total.*

Maximum points: 190   Untrained: 40+   Improver: 105+   Master: 170+

This step comprises six tests – Step 1 comprises five, so your total scores for Step 1 and Step 52 are not directly comparable. But you can compare your two scores for each individual test to see how much your memory has advanced.

Conclusion

Perhaps your sole reason for reading this book was that you felt a weakness in remembering names and faces, or shopping lists, or birthdays, or telephone numbers or PINs. Or maybe you were worried that you have been getting a little forgetful in general. Whatever your motive, I hope that you have enjoyed the challenge of developing and exercising your memory in 52 steps.

Training your memory has untold benefits. Apart from the practical advantages, you should begin to notice that your memory is becoming generally more efficient and that you have gained confidence in this ability.

When I was at school struggling to remember what I was trying to learn, I never dreamed that one day I would become a World Champion at anything, let alone memory. In fact, I had so much difficulty studying and absorbing knowledge that I left school at the earliest legal opportunity, aged sixteen. It's ironic then that many people assume that I must have been born with a special gift of recall or a photographic memory. Nothing could be further from the truth. As I have always said, mine is a trained memory. I hope that if you have a family you will pass on these skills to your children so that they can use them to study more effectively.

Memory is so important. It defines who we are and without it our lives would be in chaos. Memory training is an investment in the future well-being of your mind, and I believe strongly in the theory of "use it or lose it". Take a little time each day to exercise your memory by repeating or adapting the exercises and tests in this book for your own use. You don't have to be at your desk to do this. When you are out and about, get into the habit of employing your skills to recall names, house numbers, street names, even car registration numbers.

I find myself automatically translating numbers into images. If someone tells me their phone number, it doesn't bother me if I don't have a pen or paper handy. And I never have the embarrassment of introducing someone I have only just met but forgetting their name.

Indeed, the next time you are at a party, you should be able to remember, if you wish to, the names of everyone you meet. And as a special party piece you could always astound guests by memorizing all – or part of – a deck of playing cards.

For me, the most effective method, and one that I use daily, is the Journey Method. By now you probably have your own favourite route around your home that you use to memorize various sequences of information. You will also be able to appreciate how, with intense training, you can use the Journey Method to perform extraordinary levels of memory. Perhaps you are a potential champion yourself. If you think you might be, keep practising and maybe one day we'll be battling it out head to head for the title of World Memory Champion.

Congratulations on completing these 52 steps! And enjoy the rewards that I trust they will bring you for the rest of your life.

Further Reading

Brewer, Sarah *Simply Relax*, Ulysses Press (Berkeley, California) and Duncan Baird Publishers (London), 2000

Buzan, Tony *Make the Most of Your Mind*, Fireside (New York) and Pan (London), 1988

Buzan, Tony and **Buzan, Barry** *The Mind Map Book*, Plume Books (New York) and BBC Books (London), 1996

Buzan, Tony *The Speed Reading Book*, BBC Books (London), 2003

Buzan, Tony *Use Your Memory*, BBC Publications (New York), 1995, and BBC Books (London), 1992

O'Brien, Dominic *How to Develop a Perfect Memory*, Headline Books (London), 1993 (this book is currently out of print, but can be obtained as an ebook from www.library.com).

O'Brien, Dominic How to Pass Exams, Duncan Baird Publishers (London), 2003

O'Brien, Dominic *Learn to Remember*, Chronicle Books (New York) and Duncan Baird Publishers (London), 2000

O'Brien, Dominic *Quantum Memory Power*, Simon & Schuster Audio (New York)/ Nightingale-Conant (www. nightingale.com), 2003

Index

Contact the Author

If you would like to contact Dominic O'Brien, he can be reached through the following web address:

www.peakperformancetraining.org

Author's Acknowledgments

I wish to thank the creative team at Duncan Baird Publishers, including Bob Saxton, Justin Ford, Naomi Waters and Zoë Stone, for producing this book.